T0159096

LEADERSHIP
AND
DIVERSITY
IN
EDUCATION

An Investigation of Female Expectations in Nigeria

MICHAEL UMEADI, D.B.A., Ed.D.

authorHOUSE®

AuthorHouse™
1663 Liberty Drive
Bloomington, IN 47403
www.authorhouse.com
Phone: 1 (800) 839-8640

Published by AuthorHouse 01/20/2020

ISBN: 978-1-5462-7622-7 (sc)
ISBN: 978-1-5462-7623-4 (hc)
ISBN: 978-1-5462-7621-0 (e)

Library of Congress Control Number: 2019900450

Print information available on the last page.

This book is printed on acid-free paper.

CONTENTS

PREFACE

This book explores the gender diversity of faculty at the senior management level in public Nigerian universities. Data were collected through individual interviews and a focus group.

The sample consisted of 20 male and female faculty at the senior management level in Nigerian public universities drawn from the four geographic regions of Nigeria, namely North-Central, South-East, South-South and South-West.

Results revealed the existence of pronounced gender inequality and evidence of several factor constraints that contribute to the disproportionate representation of female and male faculty at the senior management level in public Nigerian universities. These factors were highlighted in the open, axial, and selective coding.

ACKNOWLEDGEMENT

Thank God for the power and strength to write this book. Several individuals supported or encouraged the accomplishment of this book and there may not be much space to spell out everyone, but our wish remains to recognize all those who made the completion of this book possible. Special thanks and appreciation goes to Dr. Noriega amongst others

Special thanks also must go to Mrs. Gwamniru Umeadi, my lovely wife of 30 years, who stood by me with love, devotion, and understanding through the early stage of writing. Uchenna Umeadi, Nnedi Umeadi, Chuboy Umeadi, Zora Umeadi, and Geoffrey Umeadi, who gave steadfast and invaluable support and showered understanding when research and writing kept us confined. They also deserve special thanks.

Our thanks go to the publishers, AuthorHouse publishers and all those that provided some kind of help with the manuscript for publication.

Michael Umeadi
Evelyn Lim

CHAPTER ONE

LEADERSHIP AND DIVERSITY IN EDUCATION

A leader has to understand that education provides the skills for the people of a country to survive. A leader must not only be educated and have experience, one of the major responsibilities of a leader is to ensure that the followers will receive the opportunity of gaining an education for them to succeed and sustain and improve the quality of life for other citizens of the organization or country. To enable this continuity of survival and improvement all members must receive an equal opportunity for education and upward mobility. Because of tradition and cultures in many countries and organizations those primary dimensions of diversity such as age, gender, physical abilities, etc. will often prevent some individuals from receiving certain opportunities. As countries and organizations grow, we will also see an increase in the number of some of those individuals with secondary dimensions of diversity such as education, income, religious beliefs, etc. However, in many cultures, females because of gender will not receive certain opportunities or positions as compared to those of their male counterparts. Leadership will have to accept the importance of developing an equitable environment so that individuals of all dimensions of diversity will be able to thrive.

Michael Umeadi, D.B.A., Ed.D.

Diversity in education in Nigeria

The importance of leadership in managing diversity in an organization or country is predicated on the increased workplace diversity that manifests through the different dimensions. There are various dimensions of diversity and some are primary and some are secondary (Daft, 2007). The primary dimensions of diversity include "age, gender, and race, while [the] secondary dimension[s] of diversity are education, marital status, and religion" (Daft, 2007p. 333). *Gender diversity*, which was the focus of this investigation, is a tendency to have an equal, or at least close to equal, number of employees of both genders. This tendency is also associated with benefits, such that a heterogeneous group is likely to stimulate more effectively, find quick answers to difficult questions, and look at issues from very different perspectives.

Several factors exist that stimulate *gender disparity*, including prejudice,stereotyping, and ethnicity. Norris and Wylie (2009) "cite[d] sex role stereotyping as apotential cause of discrimination and a barrier to women's movement into managerial ranks" (p. 419). Crouch (2012) indicated that elusive forms of implicit bias and prejudice have an influence in the absence of gender diversity. These factors have made it difficult to define and manage gender disparity in Nigerian universities.

Even though, "the expansion of the higher education sector has been accompanied by growing demands for greater socio-economic responsiveness on the part of universities" (Thaver&Mähick, 2008, p. 361), diversity in Nigerian universities is not at the desired level. "The ways that organizations manage workforce diversity [are] still evolving"(Carrell, Mann, & Sigler, 2006, p. 1), yet substantial evidence do not exist supporting the integration of diversity into organizations, particularly in Nigerian universities. Consequently, the disparity gender of faculty at the senior level in Nigerian universities may still be largely pronounced. Ambe-Uva, Iwuchukwu, and Jibrin (2008) indicated "men outnumber women 20 to one at senior management levels, women deans and professors are a minority group, and women vice chancellors and presidents are still a rarity" (p. 815). A World Bank (2001) report indicated "While the proportion of female students in Nigeria's federal universities has increased from 25 to 34 percent, the proportion of female academic staff has stagnated at a level of about 14 percent" (p. 4).

No exhaustive explanations have been reached surrounding the gender disparity of faculty at the senior management level in Nigerian universities. Hence, the understanding of what factors contribute to the disproportionate representation of female and male faculty at the senior management level in public Nigerian universities was the focus of the current study.

The Problem

The problem that leadership has to deal with is the gender disparity in Nigeria. The gender composition of faculty at the senior management level in public Nigerian universities indicates a pronounced level of disparity, yet the understanding of what factors contribute to the disproportionate representation of female and male faculty at this level remains unclear. It was necessary to conduct an investigation into the gender diversity of faculty at the senior management level in public Nigerian universities. The purpose of this investigation was to explore the gender diversity of faculty at the senior management level in public Nigerian universities. The research involved the use of a qualitative descriptive approach to seek the perceptions of gender disparity held by faculty at the senior management level in public Nigerian universities. Data were collected through in-depth interviews and a focus group and managed and evaluated to try and determine what were the major themes for this vast different in representation. Therefore, the issues became what factors contribute to the disproportionate representation of female and male faculty at the senior management level in public Nigerian universities? While there might have been numerous reasons for this discrepancy, examinations of the facts were important.

As with all investigations, there are usually limitations and delimitations that must be acknowledged before moving forward. The current investigation involved challenges in terms of validity, generalizable results, wider implications, and reliability. A few limitations to the investigation were related to the analysis of interview data. There was a possibility that the researcher's subjective opinions might bias the information presented or the conclusions drawn. In such cases, the investigation would become more reflective of the researchers' opinions than of the actual data, presenting issues with validity. Another significant limitation involved the ability to generalize results to other populations. Since the nature of the research method was based on perception, exploratory in nature, and tailored to the needs of one population, it would be difficult to extrapolate findings to a broader population or to draw general or far-reaching conclusions from the findings. In addition, the study was specific to one setting and was not generalizable. Consequently, it is difficult to make broad and sweeping recommendations based on the outcomes of this investigation. Of equal importance was that because the outcome of the research depended mostly on the researcher's knowledge and interpretation, it might be difficult for another researcher to obtain the same results. The new researcher might make different decisions or conduct the interviews in a different way.

Definitions

To ensure an understanding of the context and process of the investigation the authors are defining a few terms as follows:

Disproportionate representation: Lower representation from a particular group experiencing a given situation than expected based on the group's representation in the general population (Oswald & Coutinho, 2006). In the current study, disproportionate representation was used to refer to an unequal representation of gender (i.e., male and female) in public Nigerian universities.

Diversity: Differences among people in terms of age, ethnicity, gender, race, or other dimensions and a "workforce made up of people with different human qualities or who belong to various cultural groups" (Daft, 2007, p. 333). In the current study, diversity was considered in terms of the gender composition of faculty at the senior management level in public Nigerian universities.

Ethnicity: A sense of group belonging based on ideas of common origins, history, culture, language, experience, and values (Brown, 2010). In the current study, ethnicity was restricted to that contained in the country of Nigeria.

Gender: The attitudes, feelings, and behaviors that a given culture associates with a person's biological sex (American Psychological Association, 2011). In the current study, gender was viewed in terms of male versus female and masculinity versus femininity.

Gender disparity: The purely descriptive observation of different outcome between male and female (Filmer, King, & Pritchett, 1997, p. 2) associated with differences in the treatment of individuals because of gender, individual biological differences, culture, beliefs, and attitudes that play role in gender disparities. In the current study, disparity was viewed as gender inequality or a disproportionate number of male and female faculty at the senior management level in public Nigerian universities.

Gender diversity: Based on a distinction between sex and the physical characteristics that identify individuals as male or female (Schmidt, 2014, p. 1). In the current study, gender diversity was considered based on the disproportionate number of male and female faculty at the senior management level in public Nigerian universities.

Generalizable results: The degree to which the findings can be generalized from the study sample to the entire population (Polit & Hungler, 1991, p. 645), thus making predictions based on a recurring experience.

Heterogeneous management group: A group that is prone to interact more efficiently and therefore is preferred when competition is intense (Murray, 1989). In the current study, a heterogeneous management group involved equal representation of the genders for organizational effectiveness.

Prejudice: Occurs when an individual's stereotypes become rigid and inflexible (Armstrong, 2003) and reflected in the form of bias. In the current study, prejudice reflected bias against people of a particular gender. Gender bias can result indiscriminatory treatment or unequal opportunity.

Stereotyping: A standardized mental picture held in common by group members involving an oversimplified opinion or uncritical judgment (Armstrong, 2003) normally associated with type casting or labeling.

Reliability: A statistical measure of the reproducibility or stability of the data gathered (Litwin, 2003) with consistency and dependability.

Validity: An important measure of accuracy (Litwin, 2003). It involves evaluating scores on a particular test and how these scores are interpreted (Gliner & Morgan, 2000) for authenticity and rationality.

Summary

This is an important investigation as it allowed for exploring the gender diversity of faculty at the senior management level in public Nigerian universities to assist in identifying perceptions surrounding the reasons for this disparity and how the discrepancies might be eliminated. This investigation is necessary because, gender

> [u]n-representativeness may produce some negative consequences for the university system, including depriving and undercutting the academic performance of female students through the limited provision of female role models who may be more appreciative of the special challenges faced by women on campus. (World Bank, 2001, p. 4)

Consequently, the results of this investigation can be used as a guide to identify the factors that actually inhibit gender equality in Nigerian universities.The determination of these factors will enable authorities of public Nigerian universities to endorse strategies that may stimulate equality among the genders and promote stronger socio-cultural ties among the genders in the overall development of Nigerian universities. Diversity will provide a "broader and deeper base of experience for problem solving, creativity, and innovation" (Daft, 2007, p. 336).

Most importantly, the investigation will allow leaders to gain a better understanding of the status of gender diversity in education in Nigeria and to implement changes if females are to become encouraged to pursue careers in education. A leader has to understand that education is crucial to the overall development of a country and its people. Not only can education help to promote gender equality in a country, education can help to promote peace and strength. Therefore, education becomes one of the most important assets for a country's investment.

CHAPTER TWO

DIVERSITY

The leadership of Nigeria is well aware of the importance of education in order for the country to thrive and they are aware of the many perceptions of diversity that they will have to consider in the process. Therefore, the federal government primarily funds Nigeria's public universities to meet the need for a skilled workforce. Because the population of Nigeria has been increasing significantly, the capacity of the existing universities has been upgraded and new institutions have been introduced in order to meet the capacity gaps. Consequently, the number of male and female students admitted to study in the universities has grown, leading to increases in the number of faculty needed in public universities as well. Hence, it is pertinent to look at the gender diversity of the workforce (i.e., faculty) to examine whether there are concerns with the distribution of diversity among the workforce. The leadership would like to know if the culture within the individual level encompasses any identifying prejudices or stereotyping. This is essential, as leadership would like all individuals to have an equal opportunity for upward mobility within the educational system and throughout other organizations within the country.

A review of the literature was designed to focus on gender diversity in the public universities of Nigeria. The intention was to illustrate and expose the challenges associated with factors that may contribute to the disproportionate representation of female and male faculty at the senior management level in public Nigerian universities.

This task was accomplished through defining diversity, exposing the role of culture in diversity, uncovering the process of managing workforce diversity, and the role of leadership in diversity. All types of diversity are of a major concern to the leadership of Nigeria because they are concerned about having a healthy cultural environment within the country.

Concepts of Diversity

The concept of diversity is complex due to differences that exist among employees within all organizations to include educational institutions. This complexity has stimulated several definitions of diversity that differ depending on the context of the organization. In general, the definitions of diversity portray the visible and no visible differences that exist among employees in organizations. These differences can also be classified into primary and secondary dimensions. In some organizations, the primary (i.e., visible) dimensions focus on elements such as gender, age, and ethnicity while the secondary (i.e., non-visible) dimensions include elements such as religion, social class, and level of education. Nevertheless, the fundamentals of each definition consider value and respect for the differences that exist among employees in the organization. B. Y. Kim (2006), in a study about workforce diversity and learning organizations, noted that Thomas (1995): Define[d] diversity as any mixture of components characterized by similarities and differences between and among races, ages, genders, educational levels, religious affiliations, geographical origins, and work styles. Johnson and Parker (1987) regarded diversity as significant changes in the composition of the workforce such as the increasing number of women, racial minorities, senior workers, and immigrants while Cox and Blake (1991) viewed diversity as a business imperative, thus broad spectrum of variation that distinguishes among the human resources of an organization (p. 69).

Other authors and academicians have stated their perceptions of diversity. Van Es (2003) associated diversity with "age, socioeconomic background, religion,working style, family status, real-life experience, thinking style, career experience and level, sexual orientation, marital status, physical and learning disabilities, ancestry, origin, nationality, creed, color" (p. 51) and other factors. Gardenswartz and Rowe (2003) defined diversity in a visual form, one that is also largely acknowledged by other scholars (See Figure 1). They defined diversity through the diversity dimension wheel.

*Figure 1.*Diversty dimension wheel (Gardenswartz & Rowe, 2003)

The diversity dimension wheel encompasses four layers associated with organizational, external, internal, and personality dimensions. The *organizational* dimension is in the outer layer of the model, with a focus on the environment of the organization. Individual control is limited here because control rests with the organization. The characteristics include functional level or classification; management status; department, division, unit, and workgroup; union affiliation; work location; seniority; and work content or field. The *external* dimension influences diverse team behavior and the characteristics include religion, marital status, educational background, income, parental status, appearance, personal habits, recreational habits, geographic locations, and work experience. The *internal* dimension shapes the diverse team and is associated with characteristics such as age, gender, ethnicity, race, physical ability, and sexual orientation. Finally, the *personality* dimension is the inner layer of the model. It is the unique core and encompasses characteristics that include emotion, attitude, and individual behavior patterns in general.

Of equal importance, Rijamampianina and Carmichael's (2005) definition of diversity highlights a collective, all-encompassing mix of human differences and similarities along any given dimension that can be classified into primary, tertiary, and secondary dimensions. The *primary* dimensions encompass race, ethnicity, gender, age, and disability; the *secondary* dimensions are associated with religion, culture, sexual orientation, thinking style, geographic origin, family status, lifestyle, economic status, political orientation, work experience, education, language, and nationality; and the *tertiary* dimensions include beliefs, assumptions, perceptions, attitudes, feelings, values, and group norms. The dimensions of diversity are interlinked and can produce distinct human profiles associated with differences and similarities because of their interactions with and influences on one another that occur differently in different settings and situations (Rijamampianina & Carmichael, 2005). As a result, the position and dominance of each dimension is dynamic, hence making the concepts of diversity and diversity management more intricate.

There also those that provides us with a global view of diversity. Trenka (2006) defined diversity in global terms as observing people and everything that makes them different and similar from one another on the one hand, but contending that the distinguishing factors go past race and language to include such things as values and customs. Daft (2007) revealed, "Diversity refers [to] differences among people in terms of age, ethnicity, gender, race, or other dimensions" and a "workforce made up of people with different human qualities or who belong to various cultural groups" (p. 333). Hur, Strickland, and Stefanovic (2010) used the working definition of diversity as developed by Vice President Al Gore's National Partnership for Reinventing Government of "all characteristics and experiences that define each of us as individuals" (p. 500). Kapoor (2011) also reaffirmed this view.

Of equal importance, diversity in the workplace comprises increasingly diverse generations of employees. Such diversity is associated with age and reflective of a generational divide that can emerge in the workplace as well. Differences among people in terms of age occur in workplaces made up of people with different human qualities that are consistent with formative experiences ranging from World War II to World of Warcraft and create inherent problems within organizations (Daft, 2007; Meister &Willyerd, 2010). These differences in generations introduce a wide range of differences that will be of concern to organizational leaders.

The American Management Association (2014) classified the four generations that interact in the workplace based on age frame and name; those born between 1925 and 1946 as Silents, those born between 1946 and 1964 as Baby Boomers, those born between 1965 and 1980 as Generation X, and those born after 1980 as Generation Y or Millennials. These divides are now commonly found across the globe.

The Silents are the oldest generation in workplace. The Great Depression, World War II, and the postwar boom years (American Management Association, 2014) molded their Silents beliefs and moral standards. They are not risk takers, but as they believe in hard work and are committed to working together with others, they have teamwork and collaborative qualities. In addition, they are not extravagant. They have respect for authority and prefer recognition for motivation demonstrated through the practices of paying attention to employees using common courtesy, listening to employees, using powerful and positive language in interactions, putting praise in writing, and giving staff public credit for contributions (Heathfield, 2013).

This type of trait is consistent with command and control or the *authoritarian leadership style.* This leadership style is also called *autocratic leadership* and demands that workplace routines be clearly spelled out and procedural as well as clear with expectations. Decisions are made by the leader, encouraging division among leadership and employees. However, the drawback of this leadership style is its controlling and dictatorial posture, but it is appropriate in situations where time is a challenge to decision-making. This generation of workers prefers communication patterns that occur in a formal setting. Daneci-Patrau (2011) indicated communication is a tool that unites employees and upholds their relationships. The Baby Boomers are also different.

The Baby Boomers are work-oriented. They detest control, but are collegial and consensual. Their beliefs and moral standards were shaped by the rise of the Civil Rights Movement, the Vietnam War, and inflation (American Management Association, 2014). They possess democratic characteristics and are open to change. They are team players but also demand recognition. Hence, they associate themselves with leadership practices that make them feel they are doing something meaningful and provide them with effective communication and share information as well as show faith and trust in the team (Lavinsky, 2012). They prefer communication patterns consistent with the informal type,or communication that is more interpersonal in nature.

The Baby Boomer traits are consistent with the *participatory* or *democratic leadership style*. Employees under this leadership style receive guidance, and groups and their members are encouraged to fully participate and proffer input. However, leadershipis tasked with making the final decision. In addition, this style encourages engagement among group members, thereby creating motivation and creativity.

On the other hand, Generation X is self-reliant and demands work structure and direction. They are often skeptics, but possess strong technical skills and are very independent. They believe in the equality of all persons and prefer motivation strategies that emphasize an individual approach rather than consistent rules.

The Generation X trait is consistent with the *delegative leadership style*. This form of leadership style is also called *laissez-faire*. Employees under this leadership style do not receive guidance, or at best little guidance. This leadership style leaves decision making to the group, and its effectiveness is found in situations where the group members are well-educated experts in their area of endeavors. The drawback of the style is that the role of the group is poorly defined and absent of motivation.

Generation Y tend demonstrate other tendencies. Generation Y tends to be multitasking and tolerant. They greatly believe in fulfillment. This generation is educated and technologically savvy (Lowe, Levitt, &Wilson, 2011). They think short-term and prefer immediate feedback and rewards for their efforts (Lowe et al., 2011). They are, for the most part, a determined workforce and exhibit competence and accountability. They believe in hard work.

Each generation possesses different characteristics reflective of values and attitudes toward work based on its life experiences (American Management Association, 2014), which are conveyed in whole or part through communication behaviors in the organization. All of these factors affect the work environment and can spur confrontation and misunderstanding among the generations.

In combining the definitions provided by Bukhari and Sharma (2014), Kapoor (2011), Hur*et al.* (2010), Meister and Willyerd (2010), Daft (2007), Kim (2006),Rijamampianina and Carmichael (2005), Van Es (2003), Gardenswartz and Rowe (2003),and Pajares and Valiante (2001), there is evidence to show that the different forms of diversity illustrate the enormous challenges. With so many broad perceptions of diversity, leaders can have a difficult time of managing diversity in organizations or educational institutions. In addition, workplaces encompass characteristics that define individual uniqueness including attributes peculiar to gender absorbed in cultural orientation (i.e., individualistic or collectivistic formations).

Therefore, supporting this view, diversity refers to the differences stimulated by how employees perceive their workplace and the disparity associated with demographic elements that pose potential barriers to the organization. This element of disparity stimulates challenges, but when managed effectively promotes some strategic advantage to the organization. Consequently, diversity promotes organizational effectiveness along with team development and motivation.

Culture and Diversity

Leaders also have to accept the fact that culture can plays a very important part in the overall attitude in an environment as to how diversity is perceived. This perception might play a very important part in how gender diversity may be viewed. Gender diversity is a dynamic and complex phenomenon (Pajares&Valiante,2001). Loden and Rosener (1991) supported that organizational affiliation such as gender could be analyzed on three levels that include individual level factors, group or intergroup level factors (p. 7). The individual level factors encompass identity prejudice and stereotyping, while the group or intergroup level factors embrace cultural differences, ethnocentrism, and intergroup conflict.

The biases against having women in leadership positions also play an important part in the disparity of assignment. Ambe-Uva *et al.* (2008) found that gender disparity as it related to promotion (i.e., rank) within universities was largely pronounced, as "women do not occupy positions that would enable them to influence the policies and decisions of the institution at either departmental or institutional level" (p. 821).

More females are going to college and entering the field of education, Bukhari and Sharma (2014) highlighted that gender differences in the level and type of formal education and in participation in the labor force are rapidly disappearing, though the rate of advancement of women into higher positions remains relatively slow. The gender composition of faculty at the management level in public Nigerian universities shows a pronounced level of disparity.

There is also that cultural conditioning that causes a disparity in gender biases. Hence, several factors may be responsible for this pronounced level of disparity. In public Nigerian universities, as well as universities in other developing countries of sub-Saharan Africa, culture influences prejudice and stereotyping. Culture is investigated to illustrate its effect on the number of male and female faculty at the senior managementlevel in public Nigerian universities.

In countries like Nigeria, culture is a very important component in all occupations. Daft (2007) defined *culture* as a "set of key values, assumptions, understandings,and norms that is shared by members of an organization and taught to new members as correct" (p. 422). This set of factors has a direct impact on the performance of an organization. In the book, *The Leadership Experience*, Daft revealed that in their book, *Corporate Culture and Performance*, Kotter and Heskett provided evidence that "companies that intentionally managed cultural values out performed similar companies that did not" (p. 429). Because of this reasoning and the importance of culture within the country, you can see why this lifestyle of disparity in educational positions might be acceptable.

In Nigeria, various ethnic groupings are associated with some cultural dimensions. The cultural dimensions are similar to Hofstede's cultural dimensions, which are associated mostly with the power distance, individualism and collectivism, and uncertainty avoidance (Hofstede, Hofstede, & Minkov, 2010). Within this classification, the behaviors and beliefs that are considered appropriate within a culture are activated and may promote bias, negating the rise of the female gender at the senior management level. This is the development of the process of cultural prejudice and stereotyping (Chiu & Hong, 2007; Triandis & Wasti, 2008), which stimulates gender inequality. Díaz-García, González-Moreno, and Sáez-Martínez (2013), Lisowska (2009), and Churchman and Thompson (2008) support this view.

Cultural dimensions can be seen within the existing culture and values at public Nigerian universities. Power distance is dominant as the faculty may be seen as unequal in physical and intellectual capability. Individualism and collectivism are pronounced as ethnicity also exists within the cultural diversity in the university, and the dimension of uncertainty avoidance reflects the ambiguity in the different cultures and the management of such ambiguity. Consequently, gender differences in public Nigerian universities relate to social factors that are reflective of individualism and collectivism. As a result, the diversity approach is reflective of feminine (maternal) or masculine (paternal) traits, but for the most part masculinity is preferred. This diversity approach is predominant in most collectivistic cultures. Fang and Saini (2012) reported that managers in collectivistic cultures like China and India adopt paternalistic strategies to deal with diversity.

Of equal importance, the patriarchal power relations that are consistent with collectivistic cultural traits support male superiority over females, a cause for prejudice. Essien and Ukpong (2012) stated Nigeria discovered the drivers of patriarchy and gender inequality to include cultural prejudice against women. Leaders are faced with accepting this attribute of the culture and having to find an acceptable method of promoting females to higher positions.

There are also those situations where in some individual because of their cultural condition along with what they consider the norm does not want to deal with females on a congenial level. Garcia-Retamero and López-Zafra (2006) studied prejudice against women in male-congenial environments. Perceptions of gender role congruity in leadership "tested how the expectations of people affect prejudice in work environments by evaluating male or a female candidate for a leadership position in an industry with the candidates' gender role" (p. 51). They found an astonishing revelation in that participants displayed prejudice against female candidates, and "female and older participants showed more prejudice against the female leader than did male and younger participants" (p. 51).

There are also those perceptions of certain roles for females and that they should remain within those roles. Eagly Makhijani, and Klonsky (1992) found that "women in leadership positions were devalued relative to their male counterparts when leadership was carried out in stereotypically masculine styles" (p. 3). Norris and Wylie (2009) "cite[d] sex role stereotyping as a potential cause of discrimination and a barrier to women's movement into managerial ranks" (p. 419).

Some of the differences in the acceptance of cultural diversity can also be found in employee-oriented behavior. Cann and Siegfried (1990) found consideration or employee-oriented behavior and structuring or directive production-oriented behavior to be distinct behaviors that mirror differences in gender behavioral styles. Consideration qualities were associated with a feminine style, while structuring was seen as more masculine.

Similarly, Powell (2012), in a study of the intersection of gender and leadership, reached the conclusion that the managerial playing field was tilted in favor of men and associated with masculine gender stereotype behaviors, contrary to the existing phenomenon in leadership theories and field evidence consistent with developing competencies of women and men in leader roles and creating conditions that give them equal chances where leader behavior should have no gender.

In addition, Mihail (2006), in a study on gender-based stereotypes in the workplace in Greece, found the primary source of shaping respondents' attitudes to be associated with one's own gender. This result indicates characteristics like age, education, experience in management, and working under a female supervisor did not have a quantifiable effect on employees' stereotypic attitudes toward women in management. He further concluded that factors like firm nationality, ownership, sector, or department did not lead to a change in employees' attitudes.

Diekman, Goodfriend, and Goodwin (2004) found that despite the changes in gender roles, women's power role was diminished against that of men. Though the study in an open-ended report found that respondents' projections of women's power over the next 50 years would increase, responses were split equally between projecting stability and a decrease in men's power regardless of the fact that respondents alleged women as "gaining in political, economic, occupational, individual, and relational power from the past into the future" (p. 201). On the other hand, men were alleged to be decreasing in relational power, but maintained other levels and forms of power and "women were not projected to reach parity with men by 2050" (p. 201).

A substantial number of scholars have attributed stereotypes of power against women in most part to societal factors. Mirza and Jabeen (2011) found societal factors to have an impact on both the individual and organizational levels in continuing the existing stereotyping against both genders, consequently deterring the progress of women in their professions.

The views encompassed above clearly support that stereotyping originates from particular gender bias that may be the result of culture. There is evidence to suggest that the collectivistic cultural composition of countries of sub-Saharan Africa tend to lean masculine and expose women as the weak gender. Hence, stereotyping is traceable to such culture composition.

The consequence of stereotyping is that it brings about gender disparity. It inhibits the potential of one gender to participate effectively in various capacities and sectors of the economy, including the education sector. In addition, it may inhibit promotions and the rise of one gender to managerial positions in educational institutions, particularly in Nigerian universities. Stereotyping is a dominant factor (Ambe-Uva et al., 2008) that may inhibit gender promotions and rapid rise into managerial positions in educational institutions, particularly in Nigerian universities.

The substantial support found for the effect of culture in the diversity of an organization was the basis for provoking the current exploration into the gender disparity among male and female faculty in public Nigerian universities. The findings of Crouch (2012), Norris and Wylie (2009), Ambe-Uva et al. (2008), and Daft (2007) clearly show culture influences prejudice and stereotyping. Ayub, Aslam, Razzaq, Iftekhar, andHafeez (2013), Rai (2012), and Gathers (2003) support this view as well.

This represents a predominant factor of interest in the current investigation into the reason why gender disparity exists in Nigerian universities. However, organizations, including educational institutions, engage in a variety of initiatives to manage cultural differences, prompting the need for a greater understanding of the specific factors that promote disparity in public Nigerian universities.

Managing Diversity

A leader has the responsibility of managing diversity in order to reach organizational effectiveness and to ensure equality for all. Managing diversity is all about creating value from human differences and similarities. It also encompasses the values that motivate individual employees that enable diverse people to work as a team, driving innovation and creativity, strengthening leadership capabilities and skills, and enhancing the ability to identify and create new opportunities.

Workplace diversity is also about building and upholding a positive work atmosphere or setting in which similarities and differences inherent within a diverse group are taken into account, enabling the diverse group to exhibit its full potential and contribute to the benefit of the institutional planned objectives. Diversity draws to mind the importance of employment equity and affirmative action. Although the complexity of diversity management has led to differing views regarding the relationships between diversity management, employment equity, and affirmative action, scholars comprehend the concept of diversity management as identical to employment equity and affirmative action and use them interchangeably.

Related to the relationships between diversity management, employment equity, and affirmative action, Rijamampianina and Carmichael (2005) acknowledged their differences, but argued that managing diversity effectively hinges on the application of employment equity, while the application of employment equity depends on the effective implementation of diversity management.

In support of the above, it is therefore necessary to indicate that employment equity, affirmative action, and diversity management complement each other and should be integrated if diversity is to be made an asset in organizations, including public educational institutions. The differences and similarities are better managed through a management system and workplace designed to stimulate "employment equity programs" (Rijamampianina & Carmichael, 2005), predicating that a formidable association exists between leadership and diversity. Figure 2 illustrates the differences between employment equity and diversity management.

Employment Equity	Diversity Management
• Changes the way an organization looks	• Changes the way an organization works
• Changes the mix of people	• Changes the mix of people, environment, systems, processes…
• Focuses only on differences	
	→empowerment
	→transformation
• Focuses on race, gender and disabilities	• Focuses on both differences and similarities
• Anti-discrimination	• Focuses on all dimensions
• An end in itself	of diversity
• Externally driven	
• Legally mandated; social and moral justification	• Pro-inclusivity
	• The means to an end
	• Internally driven
	• Voluntary; a business imperative

*Figure 2.*Differences between employment equity and diversity management (Rijamampianina & Carmichael, 2005, p. 109).

Of equal importance, workplace diversity portrays functionalist perspectives that observe workplace diversity as being associated with organizational effectiveness through a focus on leadership, communication (Ayub et al., 2013), and motivation. Therefore, leaders of public Nigerian universities and organizations in general wanting to successfully integrate a diverse team of employees in their workplace may also promote the various leadership strategies geared toward studying the diverse group or team. This can be achieved by embracing an adequate leadership style that is suitable to moving the organization forward.

Consequently, the need for a stronger leadership role and an organizational culture that may begin to address and resolve diverse workforce issues connected with prejudice and stereotyping in public Nigerian universities becomes pertinent. An adequate leadership role and organizational culture may decrease the organizational challenges that affect how organizations recruit employees, communicate, and motivate diverse groups. Indeed, these characteristics shape and define the whole atmosphere in the organization. Managerial efforts and other contextual variables moderate the relationship between diversity and organizational outcomes (Choi & Rainey, 2010, p. 109).

Summary

It is obvious that there is a wide variety of perceptions of what the true definition of diversity is and how the perceptions of it can have several different levels of meaning. Along with this, the introduction of different generations into this pool of perceptions provides even more attributes to evaluate when considering the complexity of it. However, when it comes to gender, we have more agreement on the specificity of it and can agree on how the context of this conversation when it comes to inequality is not a new one. The major problem that comes into play in the discussion of diversity and upward mobility in education and other career fields often comes down to accepted premises and cultural conditioning. Therefore, it will becomes the problem of leadership to try and ensure that this age old problem of gender preferences for certain levels of management and leadership is eradicated and for leaders to provide avenues for gender equality.

CHAPTER THREE

LEADERSHIP THEORIES AND PROCESSES

A number of theories of leadership have evolved over time, allowing many more to emerge. Daft (2007) classified leadership theories into six main approaches to include the Great Man theory, trait theory, behavior theory, contingency theory, influence theory,and relational theory.

The *Great Man theory* maintains the understanding that leaders are born with inherent leadership abilities and attributes, the *trait theory* underscores that leaders possess distinct traits; the *behavior theory* emphasizes the role of a leader and consequently begins to determine leadership effectiveness based on behavior, and the *contingency theory* emphasizes situational factors. Such situational factors, according to Daft (2007), include "the characteristics of followers, characteristics of the work environment and follower tasks, and the external environment" (p. 22). The focus of the *influence theory* is on charismatic leadership, while the *relational theory* focuses on transformational and servant leadership.

As they evolved, the early leadership theories converged to develop applicable leadership theories focused on the motivation of followers. One such theory is the Level 5 leadership theory (Collins, 2001). Benson (2015) noted Kouzes and Posner revealed the "leadership best practices" (p. 3) and the "five practices common to personal-best leadership as model the way, inspire a shared vision, challenge the process, enable others to act and encourage the heart related to motivating the employee in reference to inspiration, encouragement and empowerment" (p. 4).

The theories of leadership have also promoted several aspects of the definition of leadership. Generally, the definitions tend to concur with each other. One definition indicates that leadership is the ability to inspire other people with a dream. Another definition indicates that the process of leading people in the right direction in order to achieve goals. Others indicate that the action that directs the followers to lead a respectable and honorable life. In addition, there is the thought that the relation and behavior of leaders toward their followers, is a process in which one person encourages, inspires, and motivates others to work for the betterment of society. O'Toole (2010) would support this view.

General James V. Edmundson (Puryear, 1978) defined leadership within the aspect of patterns of relationships that include relations with superiors (loyalty and industry), relationships that encompass honesty and professional knowledge, relationships with contemporaries, and the relationship of man with himself.

The various but similar opinions present an interesting dilemma for researchers and the quest to continue to find a more suitable definition for the art of leadership. Consequently, *leadership* can be defined as the capacity to influence, guide, and direct subordinates and employees toward a clear vision of the company for better results. Such leadership capacity demands individuals with strong personalities and good instincts that are able to stimulate cordial relationships and encompass character, patriotism, responsibility, dedication, and commitment. Daft (2007) stated, "Leadership is an influence relationship among leaders and followers who intend real changes and outcomes that reflect their shared purposes" (p. 4).

The characteristic of effective diversity management is associated with leadership patterns and styles as well. The leadership pattern and style enables the provision of direction, implementing plans, and motivating employees (Bakotié, 2008). Leadership styles vary depending on different organizational experiences. Their effectiveness depends on the needs of the organization (e.g., educational institution) and the makeup of the group being led (e.g., diverse group).

Lewin, Lippitt, and White (1939) identified major leadership styles to include authoritarian or autocratic, participative or democratic, and delegative or free reign. Most leadership styles are geared toward the technique of leading change in an organization, some leaders use all three styles with one of them being normally dominant, while others tend to stick to one style. The complexity in leadership styles and the quest to find the leadership style that is most adequate to bring the best outcome have stimulated several scholastic debates.

Wageeh, Nile, and Belal (2012) addressed two issues—the evaluative attitudes of employees toward leadership style and organizational learning—and the relationship between leadership style and organizational learning. They found differences among three groups of employees and found leadership styles have significant direct effects on organizational learning.

Bakotié (2008) classified leadership style into job-based as exploitive authoritative or benevolent-authoritative leadership style and employee-based as consultative or participative group leadership style. In an authoritative leadership style, employees are not consulted for any part of decision-making, but simply receive orders without explanation. Full powers rest with the leadership and employee motivation is found in a structured set of rewards and punishments. Though this kind of leadership style seems rigid, it does emanate in situations where the employee is new to the job and the leader is competent and has full knowledge of required tasks. A participative group leadership style occurs mostly when the leader and the led work together as a team to achieve organizational goals.

Similarly, Lee and Low (2012) found that the transformational leadership style has a significant positive relationship with subordinates' organizational citizenship behavior, whereas the transactional leadership style negatively relates to organizational citizenship behavior. Organizational citizenship behavior describes subordinates' (i.e., employees) voluntary commitment within the organization that is not part of the contractual tasks. It is a specific type of leadership that leads to higher job satisfaction and commitment. In addition, inspirational appeals and consultation tactics, as downward influence tactics, a form of pressure tactics (i.e., assertiveness), were found to mediate the relationship between transformational leadership and organizational citizenship behavior. Subordinates' competence mediates the relationship between transformational leadership and consultation tactics.

The dimensions of the individual level factors and group or intergroup level factors associated with diversity impose barriers that inhibit organizational effectiveness. Consequently, gender disparity, which may be influenced by culture, makes cultural differences in communication in the workplace, including in public Nigerian universities, more significant.

Accordingly, leadership competence in diversity management would also depend on the leadership strategy encompassing a variety of initiatives that enhance organizational performance. Such initiatives are influenced by the leadership style at the levels of communication, team building, and motivation.

Communication

Approaches and theories clarify and affect organizational communication in the workplace. The functional and meaning-centered approaches place emphasis, respectively, on the importance of communication in organizational efficiency as well as employee interactions in the workplace in relation to culture (Shockley-Zalabak, 2011).

Similarly, the postmodern theory acknowledges organizing, relationship, and change messages; the critical theory seeks to improve relations within the organization to facilitate feelings among employees that they have a stake in the organization; while the feminist theory emphasizes recognition and valuing the participation of all, including women, minorities, and others (Shockley-Zalabak, 2011). Generally, the postmodern, critical, and feminist perspectives are integrated and emphasize the power and control that inhibit effective communication in the workplace (Ogbor, 2001).

The importance of communication in organizations is critical and largely emphasized. *Communication* refers to the transfer of message interpersonally and among groups. It can be used as a tool to unite employees (Shockley-Zalabak, 2011) and boost organizational efficiency. Consequently, the result of a diverse group in an organization may cause the flow of information to be distorted. Indeed, the problem more often occurs in the interaction stage between the genders. Therefore, the structure of the organization dictates the communication pattern (Shockley-Zalabak, 2011).

Communication patterns occur in both formal and informal settings. Extensive research has considered the relationship between formal and informal communication. Scholars such as Kandlousi, Ali, and Abdollahi (2010) found formal and informal communication predicted communication satisfaction. Daneci-Patrau (2011) indicated communication to be tool that unites diverse groups of employees and upholds their relationships.

In public Nigerian universities, communication flows within the prescribed channels of formal communication. Formal communication predicates the exchange of messages concerning official work. Its occurrence is normally through official channels of message flow between university positions. The formal communication flow pattern provides directions associated with downward communication, upward communication, and horizontal communication.

> *Downward communication* is the most common form of communication. The process of information flow is from the authority level to subordinates. This communication process is consistent with the flow of information prescribing directions, instruction, and information to the university members. Messages are usually transmitted using technology (e.g., e-mail, telephone) or in face-to-face settings, such as meetings.
>
> *Upward communication* is the reverse to downward communication. It is associated with information flow starting from the subordinates to the authority level of the university based on hierarchy. This kind of communication provides feedback and

information up the university hierarchy. This communication
process tends to motivate employees.

Horizontal communication facilitates problem solving and information
sharing across different work groups. The process is consistent
with information flow among subordinates or employees. Its
advantage is that of direct communication among employees
to enhance coordination.

Informal communication does not reflect officially designated
channels of communication in the workplace, but is the exchange of
unofficial messages that are unrelated to formal workplace activities.
It emerges from the social and personal interests of employees rather
than formal requirements of the workplace. Informal communication
does not maintain superior–subordinate relationships, rather it is direct,
spontaneous, and flexible (Rayudu, 2010, p. 25). The advantage of this
communication process is that employees may use it for relaxation,
which may enhance productivity. However, the drawback is that when
abused, informal communication can forestall job efficiency and
productivity.

The importance of interpersonal communication has also been
stressed. Popescu (2013) noted interpersonal communication drives
the process of the professional development of individual employees
through the transmission and exchange of information. Sethi and Seth
(2009) noted interpersonal communication is the "procedure by which
people swap information, feelings and impart through verbal and nonverbal messages" (p. 32). Interpersonal communication is the process
of communication that allows for the flow of information between
individuals, enabling understanding and fostering relationship.

Verbal and nonverbal communication processes are used within
interpersonal communication. Verbal communication is associated with
writing and speaking, while nonverbal communication is consistent
with body language and facial expressions.

Language is a factor in the verbal communication process that
can prompt misunderstandings during interpersonal communication.

Therefore, interpersonal communication must be effective to be meaningful. "Listening; asking questions; discussing; sharing information; agreeing; suggesting; getting feedback; answering questions and explaining" (Keyton et al., 2013, p. 152) are all effective verbal communication behaviors.

In public Nigerian universities at the departmental level, interpersonal communication occurs in both one-way and two-way process. The *one-way communication* process usually occurs when the Head of the department stops by the departmental administrative assistant to pass along information about a likely assignment or project due date. This kind of communication process is quick for the transmitter and does not orchestrate disagreement from the recipient. *Two-way communication* is the sharing of information constructively between two or more parties. In this kind of communication process, the Head of the department would hold faculty meetings to establish the timelines and due dates for a number of assignments and projects. Engaging in two-way communication indicates that the transmitter is receptive to feedback and willing to provide a response.

In order to effectively manage diversity in public Nigerian universities, leadership needs to possess communication competence to cultivate a work environment that exposes employees to a high level of "interaction, visioning and learning process" (Rijamampianina & Carmichael, 2005, p. 113). The interaction process is associated with employees reaching the capacity to take competition as well as promoting a feeling of cooperation. The visioning process enables employees to cultivate the ability to adopt the organizational vision as their own, and the learning process involves employees to the level where they can share and exchange information, knowledge, skills, and competencies for the common goals of the organization. All of this is associated with leadership capacity to manage, as effective communication improves decision-making and the quality of decisions.

Of equal importance, managing diversity has important ethical ramifications for the organization (Ayub et al., 2013). Consequently, in managing diversity in public Nigerian universities, the relationship between ethics and values needs to be recognized. Values are the amalgam of attitudes that influence individual behavior during interactions. They are standards that guide ongoing activities as well as guides for decision-making (Deloris, 2003). Ethics are standards by which such behaviors are evaluated to ascertain what is right or wrong (Hill, 2012). As a result, individual value systems affect the morality of a particular behavior.

The value systems of individuals and organizations are conveyed through communication behaviors. The organizational values are revealed in the organization's mission statement and in the decision-making process. This process is modified and conveyed through organizational communication processes. As a result, it influences all decision-making and employee behaviors.

Decision-making and problem-solving can be influenced by a single leader. For the most part, the leader's mandates govern the decision-making and problem-solving processes. The leader of a group makes a decision and announces the decision to the group (Shockley-Zalabak, 2011). However, for decisions to be effective and problems to be resolved, communication must be thorough and accurate.

Some barriers can inhibit the decision-making and problem-solving processes. Shockley-Zalabak (2011) identified decision-making and problem-solving barriers as organizational barriers, task and procedural barriers, and interpersonal barriers. In public Nigerian universities, interpersonal barriers manifest in the form of poor leadership or a variety of self-centered or ego-centered behavior that negatively influences the group and poses potential behaviors that suspend critical thinking.

Because organizational culture and values influence the decision-making and problem-solving processes, the consensus model of decision-making is advocated. This model is consistent with members agreeing on what is best and supporting the decision (Shockley-Zalabak, 2011). Consequently, the organizational culture of the university should be set up in a way that allows all genders the right to excel for the good of the organization.

Organizational structure and policies can encourage the decentralization of decision-making, stimulate upward feedback, and dissimulate organizational silence, which can retard change and development and inhibit effective decision-making as well as contribute to low commitment, trust, and openness (Shockley-Zalabak, 2011). Inaddition, low quality decision-making and problem solving can manifest because of an inadequate definition of the problem and the inability to organize meetings and enable contribution from qualified faculty in brainstorming to seek improvement. Inadequate descriptions of problems and other procedural issues relate to low-quality decisions (Shockley-Zalabak, 2011).

Team Management and Building

Workplace diversity also characterizes the critical perspective surrounding gender disproportion in the workplace that reflects non-inclusiveness (Ayub et al., 2013) and limits female faculty's opportunities to access senior management levels. The critical perspective, which focuses on understanding the inner workings of organizations or educational institutions, exposes the systemic inequities that exist at multiple levels of the organization. Such inequities include hiring, promotions, and placements. These inequities may inhibit workplace diversity. Consequently, the need for leadership to stimulate diversity of thought in the employees or teams is pertinent. A good starting point is to have an accomplished team.

Management of cultural differences in gender diversity may not necessarily be shaped through compliance with the Equal Employment Opportunity (EEO) legislation regulations alone. However, nurturing an unbiased workforce will have the tendency to stimulate the diverse group into a team where the potential of each will be adequately realized and utilized. Hence, diversity is the main element for building teams. Daft(2007) revealed that in their book, *Corporate Culture and Performance*, Kotter and Heskett provided "evidence that companies that intentionally managed cultural values outperformed similar companies that did not" (p. 429).

Most organizational success depends on the ability to build teams as well as to interact with others on that team. Effective teams possess certain qualities that provide for the ability to align the team with the vision of the organization. By losing organizational vision, a team can lose the whole purpose of coming together. Hence, an effective team is usually committed to the vision of the organization. A team may not be committed to the vision of the organization if it is not adaptable to each other, energetic, enthusiastic, and selfless as well as driven by a shared purpose, thus knowing their work, tasks, duties, contributions, roles, responsibilities, and impacts to the organization. Consequently, a team is most appropriate when the organizational problem to be addressed is complex with team members having a high degree of interdependence (Sheard & Kakabadse, 2004) devoid of prejudice and stereotyping.

The effectiveness of team quality is built through communication, trust, and innovative mentality. Communication is the panacea to clear bonding of the team and allows the members to stay as intimate allies through the mission of fulfilling the organizational goals. Team members freely share ideas, opinions, and possible results. An effective team introduces a feedback forum, such as gatherings where feedback on performance, ideas, and needs is communicated and reviewed. A breakdown in communication can spur team conflicts. One such conflict can arise from a lack of respect among team members. In addition, trust is a formidable quality of a team. An effective team must be consistent with its objectives and goals and accountable to thesame standard. Effective teams possess an innovative mentality and constantly search for ways to improve the organization.

Every effective and good team is usually because of a great, visionary leader. Leadership strives to assemble an interconnected team by removing individual competition among team members, delegating, clearly defining the reporting structure, creating team incentive for excellence, defining expectations and excellence clearly, providing professional development opportunities, giving the team the power to make and implement decisions, tackling team conflict immediately, and encouraging open and honest discussion. Through the development phases of task and relationship behavior, organizations become a true, synergistic team (John & William, 2001).

Teamwork grows organizations. In managing team diversity, more emphasis is placed on teamwork (Horwitz, 2005). The knowledge of various compositional effects of team diversity on performance helps organizations determine how to align diverse teams with their strategic goals and enhance overall organizational performance.

Though the quality and effectiveness of teams are largely dependent on members' unique characteristics and strengths, a synergistic effect of individual characteristics on team performance may be achieved through coordinating and integrating diversity into one cohesive entity (Horwitz, 2005).

Team diversity is a dynamic and complex phenomenon. The best organizations bring together great employees saddled with the best knowledge, intelligence, and creativity, but will not succeed if there is no teamwork. In a diverse workplace, team conflict is inevitable if the roles and responsibilities of the diverse team members are unclear. Conflict can emerge between members of the team that is increasingly characterized by differences in core values and socio-cultural identities. However, the effective use of a team to harness the benefit of their differences and similarities becomes necessary. Therefore, in organizations, if all team members are not on the same page, dysfunction can set in.

Team dysfunction can erupt as a result of the absence of trust, fear of conflict, and lack of commitment. In the absence of trust, team members may begin to conceal weaknesses and mistakes from one another and not provide constructive feedback. In some circumstances, team members hold grudges and even dread meetings as well as find reasons to avoid staying together with team members. Similarly, when fear of conflict manifests within team members, artificial harmony is stimulated and team members pay no attention to contentious topics that would otherwise help the team's success and growth. Of equal importance, a lack of commitment among team members can lead to ambiguity or doubt. It can also bring about issues that will breed a lack of confidence and fear of failure and support second-guessing among team members.

Team dysfunction can be overcome with strong leadership. In the absence of trust, the leadership strategy should be open to conversing freely and recognizing the strengths and weaknesses of team members. The immense power of trust makes it a critical part of the peace building process that can be integrated into interventions in conflict resolution. Communication is a fundamental activity for trust building. A leadership option can be accept openly with a team member when the member is more skilled in a specific area or qualified for a particular position regardless of gender.

Similarly, when fear of conflict manifests within team members, leadership's best option is to demand debate and thus recognize the importance of conflict for productive meetings, stressing more openness and creating basic rules for engaging in conflict, as well as identifying the natural conflict style of individual team members.

The role of leadership in a lack of commitment among team members is to enforce clarity and closure through the review of the commitment of team members at the end of each meeting and bring them together and closer. Making sure that team members are committed regardless of their disagreement, thus embrace when they disagree and attempt to develop a commit mentality.

Motivating for change

Leadership will have to motivate employees to change attitudes and perceptions in order for the employees to understand the positive impact equality can have on the educational institution and the country as a whole. The problem of how to motivate employees to reach such organizational objectives remains a major concern in many organizations. According to Daft (2007), "Motivation refers to the forces either internal or external to a person that arouse enthusiasm and persistence to pursue a certain course of action" (p. 227).Similarly, Benson (2015) noted that Kinicki and Kreitner "defined motivation as those of psychological processes that caused the arousal, direction, and persistence of voluntary actions that are goal directed"(p. 4).

According to Daft (2007),"Leaders can use motivation theory to help satisfy follower's needs and simultaneously encourage high work performance" (p. 227).Such major motivational theories include Maslow's theory of the hierarchy of needs, Herzberg's two-factor theory and McClelland's acquired need theory. "Maslow's theory proposes that humans are motivated by multiple needs and those needs exist in a hierarchical order: physiological (food), safety, belongingness, esteem and self-actualization" (Daft, 2007, p. 230).

Herzberg's two-factor theory encompasses two sets of factors for employee motivation––hygiene and motivators. The *hygiene factors* include the work environment, salary, policies, procedures, and the relationship between the leader and follower; while the *motivator factors* address issues pertaining to achievement, recognition, responsibility, and the opportunity to grow (Herzberg, Mausner, & Snyderman, 1959).

McClelland's (1988) acquired need theory emphasizes three individual needs: theneed for achievement, power, and affiliation. The theory recognizes individual differences and suggests that to properly motivate employees; leadership must understand first and foremost the needs of the employees and develop a work environment that promotes motivation.

The understanding of what leadership and motivation represent through these theories definitely helps further the understanding of some general principles of human behavior. Effective leadership conversant with human behavior makes employees feel important and appreciated and creates opportunities to provide rewards and recognition to employees. Consequently, apart from providing the vision and directions to followers, a key leadership trait is the ability to inspire followership. Effective leadership may inspire followership through building relationships with employees. Hence, successful leaders inspire employees to feel important and become more effective. This is accomplished by adopting an all-inclusive policy that recognizes gender diversity as well as all other dimensions of diversity.

Although the recognition of employees can be demonstrated through practices that include paying attention to employees, using common courtesy and positive language in interactions, keeping commitments to employees, providing employees with effective communication and sharing information, and showing faith and trust in the team (Heathfield, 2013; Lavinsky, 2012), it is also pertinent to recognize that employee commitment involves the levels of obligation, belonging, and ownership (Rijamampianina & Carmichael, 2005). Hence, there is a need to manage the motivational process.

Managing the motivational process is principally designed to increase each individual employee's commitment at the ownership level (Rijamampianina & Carmichael, 2005). The increase in the ownership level of employees helps raise their performance to the best of their abilities. However, creating such an attitude of ownership is not simple, as it requires that leadership ensure fairness in the management system and the work environment. Rijamampianina and Carmichael (2005) highlighted an open and equal opportunity environment, transparency in the implementation of the policies, and delegation of responsibilities as keys to influencing the "interaction process,visioning process and the learning process" (p. 112) consistent with the process of creating some sense of ownership in organizations, including in public Nigerian universities.

However, the fact remains that leaders will have to influence and motivate individuals to understand the acceptance of diversity for the benefit of overall effectiveness of the organization or country. Motivations is an essential key that leaders must invoke in order to draw attend to the issue of diversity and the importance of dealing with it. If motivating is not encouraged individuals with have a tendency to become satisfied with the status quo.

Summary

A review of the literature pertaining, diversity, leadership and the cultural climate toward educational staffing in Nigeria was very informative. The review provided an analysis of the gender diversity of faculty at the senior management level in public Nigerian universities, the key aspect of the study. The review was grounded by defining diversity, uncovering the role of culture in diversity, exposing the process of managing diversity, and exploring the role of leadership in diversity.

As evidenced by their definitions of diversity, Bukhari and Sharma (2014),Kapoor (2011), Hur et al. (2010), Meister and Willyerd (2010), Daft (2007), Kim (2006), Rijamampianina and Carmichael (2005), Van Es (2003), Gardenswartz and Rowe (2003),and Pajares and Valiante (2001) clearly showed that diversity refers to individual uniqueness and differences, disparity associated with demographic elements such asgender, and challenges associated with managing diversity. The challenges of managing diversity are associated with factors that contribute to the disproportionate representationof female faculty, leading to gender disparity at the senior management level in public Nigerian universities.

Culture and its role in the diversity shows that gender differences in public Nigerian universities may also relate to social factors that are reflective of individualism and collectivism and hence reflective of feminine (maternal) or masculine (paternal) traits respectively. The findings of Crouch (2012), Norris and Wylie (2009), Ambe-Uvaet al. (2008), Daft (2007), Ayub et al. (2013), Rai (2012), and Gathers (2003) clearly show that culture influences prejudice and stereotyping.

Consequently, culture induced prejudice and stereotyping may be among the root causes of gender disparity among male and female faculty in public Nigerian universities.The decision for organizations, including educational institutions, to engage in a varietyof initiatives to manage cultural differences further promotes the need for a greater understanding of culture.

Managing diversity focuses on maximizing the ability of all employees to contribute to organizational goals. The characteristic of effective diversity managementis associated with leadership patterns and styles as well. The leadership pattern and style enable the provision of direction, implementing plans, and motivating employees (Bakotié, 2008). Such initiatives are influenced by the leadership style as it relates to communication, team building, and motivation. Consequently, the need for stronger leadership role and an organizational culture that may begin to address and resolve diverse workforce issues becomes pertinent. Hence, the purpose of this investigation was to explore the gender diversity of faculty at the senior management level in public Nigerian universities. The importance of this to the leaders of Nigeria cannot be understated.

CHAPTER FOUR

INVESTIGATIVE PROCESS

The investigation was guided by a qualitative phenomenological approach to explore perceptions of the phenomenon (Madden, 2008) of the gender diversity of facultyat the senior management level in public Nigerian universities. Qualitative research is an"inquiry process of understanding a social or human problem, based on building acomplex holistic picture with words" (Creswell, 1998, p. 1). Qualitative research is usually undertaken to generate knowledge and contribute to scholarship, policy, practice,and generally to the good of participants.

However, in conducting such research, tension is often created between the aims of researcher to make generalizations for the good of others and the rights of the participants to maintain privacy. The protection of participants through the informed consent process favors a formalized interaction between researcher and participant. The strength of qualitative research methods often lies in the informality of the communication as well as the iterative nature of the research process.

The obligation to inform participants that they are part of a research project is considered universal. Researchers are responsible for ensuring that participants or their representatives are given sufficient opportunity to consider whether to participate and must seek to avoid coercion or implied overt and covert or undue influence (ArgosyUniversity, 2012, p. 25). The broadcasting of qualitative research results must be done in a way that protects participant confidentiality and disallows retribution.

In qualitative research, several ethical principles are used, including autonomy, beneficence, and justice (Hennink, Hutter, & Bailey, 2011). *Autonomy* emphasizes the need to have appropriate consent and assent from participants. Consent to participate should be obtained under circumstances where participants have reasonable time to listen to the investigator's explanation and the participant's physical, mental, and psychological state must not impede the comprehension of information or the ability to make a rational and non-coerced choice (Argosy University, 2012, p. 24). *Beneficence* requires that participants' identities be kept confidential to ensure they are protected from harm. *Justice* is promoted when the researcher allows participants to review their transcripts and data interpretations. Ethical dilemmas are resolved by adopting these principles.

In order to investigate the gender diversity of faculty at the senior management level in public Nigerian universities, a primary research question was developed: *What factors contribute to the disproportionate representation of female and male faculty at the senior management level in public Nigerian universities?*

Interview questions were developed and evolved from the study rationale and purpose and guided the research. The interview questions were presented to male and female faculty at the senior management level in Nigerian universities drawn on site from four public universities in the four geographic regions of Nigeria; namely, North-Central, South-East, South-South, and South-West. Probes were used to explore the topics in more depth.

Selection of Participants

There are two main classifications of sampling methods: probability and non-probability. In a *probability* sample, each member of the population has a known non-zero probability of being selected. Probability sample methods include random sampling, systematic sampling, stratified sampling, and cluster sampling. The obvious advantage of probability sampling is that *sampling error*, or the degree to which a sample might differ from the population, can be calculated. Its disadvantage is the method is quite expensive. *Nonprobability* sample methods include convenience sampling, snowball sampling, theoretical sampling, and typical sampling. In non-probability sampling, members are selected from the population in some nonrandom manner.

In qualitative studies, nonprobability purposeful or criterion-based sampling is the type most often used because their characteristics are applicable or related to the research questions (Hennink et al., 2011). Consequently, the strategy is usually associated with the research questions or purpose, study time frame, and availability of resources (Hennink et al., 2011).

Nonprobability purposeful sampling strategies are associated with various qualitative traditions that include case study, phenomenology, ethnography, grounded theory, and narrative. Such nonprobability purposeful sampling also includes the convenience sample, snowball sample, theoretical sample, and typical sample (Henninket al., 2011). Each of these sample techniques has strengths and weaknesses, or advantages and disadvantages.

The advantages of a convenience sample are associated with such factors as time, money, and location and this type of sample is associated with the various qualitative traditions. However, disadvantages include questions surrounding credibility and the gathered information is not very rich. The advantage of the snowball sample technique is in participant referral characteristics of sample selection. The participants are identifiable by the researcher. This technique is best used in phenomenology and narrative qualitative traditions, but the disadvantage is associated with a large sample size resulting from continuous referrals. The advantage of the theoretical sample is that samples are chosen as the study progresses. It is best used in grounded theory qualitative tradition. However, the disadvantage is that the sample size grows as the study continues to stretch.The typical sampling is reflective of the average representative of the phenomenon of interest. It has no significantly different characteristics and can be used in case study, phenomenology, ethnography, and narrative qualitative tradition. For the purpose of investigating the gender diversity of faculty at the senior management level in public Nigerian universities, a typical sampling method was used.

Sample Selection

Four public universities in the four geographic regions of Nigeria (i.e., North-Central, South-East, South-South, and South-West) were selected for the purpose of exploring the gender diversity of faculty at the senior management level in public Nigerian universities. The universities were Abuja University; The University of Nigeria, Nsukka, Federal University, Otuoke; and University of Ibadan. The four universities were selected with consideration for accessibility, as they were within a convenient transportation route for the researcher and were easily reachable. The study settings are described below.

Abuja University is in Abuja, the capital of Nigeria, and is in the north central region of Nigeria. The university was established in 1988 and began academic work 2years later in 1990. The university has both conventional and distance learning programs and offers diplomas as well as undergraduate and postgraduate degrees. The university is located in a permanent site that covers about 11,824 hectares. Apart from the permanent site, the university has a mini campus in Gwagwalada, Abuja. The permanent site is home to the faculty of arts, science, veterinary medicine, and agriculture, college of medicine, and the university's senate and other administrative building. The faculty of social science, management, and law are in the mini campus. The university also has a consultancy services sub-degree program and an institute of education. The Vice chancellor of the university is male.

The University of Nigeria, Nsukka is a public university owned by the Nigerian federal government and is in the South-East zone of Nigeria. The university was founded in1955 and formally opened in October of 1960. The university has four campuses, the main campus in Nsukka and three other mini campuses in Enugu town, Ituku-Ozalla town, and Aba town, all in the eastern part of Nigeria. The main campus of the University of Nigeria is located on 871 hectares of hilly savannah in the town of Nsukka with an additional 209 hectares of arable land available for an experimental agricultural farm and 207 hectares for faculty and staff housing development. The University of Nigeria, Nsukka is the first land-grant university in Africa and one of the five elite universities in Nigeria. The university has 15 faculties and 102 academic departments. It offers 82 undergraduate programs and 211 postgraduate programs. The main campus, the Nsukka campus, houses the faculties of agriculture, arts, biological sciences, education, engineering, pharmaceutical sciences, physical sciences, social sciences, and veterinary medicine. The vice chancellor is male.

Federal University, Otuoke, is a federal government university that was established in 2011. The university is located in Otuoke, Bayelsa State, in the South-South geographic zone of Nigeria in the oil-rich Niger-Delta region. The university is located on 200 hectares or 494 acres of land. The university offers degree courses at the undergraduate level. Presently, the university has two academic faculties: humanities and social sciences, and science (i.e., engineering & technology). The student population at the university is 300 and is expected to grow gradually to a maximum size of 6,000 students over a 10- to 15-year period. The Vice chancellor (president) of the university is male.

The University of Ibadan is located in Ibadan, Oyo state, in the South-West zone of Nigeria and is the oldest and one of the most prestigious Nigerian universities. The university is located on 5 miles or 8 kilometers of land. The university is the home of a college of medicine and 10 other faculties: arts, science, agriculture and forestry, social sciences, education, veterinary medicine, technology, law, public health, and dentistry. The Vice chancellor (president) of the university is male.

Instrumentation

Interviews. Interviews were the primary method used to answer the qualitative research question. Various forms of interview design exist for obtaining thick, rich data(Creswell, 2007). Notably, some of the forms include informal conversational, general interview guide approach, and standardized open-ended interview.

Interview preparations include certain elements. A pilot test is one such element of interview preparation. Pilot tests assist in determining flaws, limitations, and weaknesses within the interview design and allow for revisions to be made prior to the implementation of the study (Kvale, 2007). Pilot tests must be conducted with sample participants with similar interests as those in the implemented study and can greatly assist in the refinement of research questions (Turner, 2010).

However, for the current study, the interview questions were created using an expert panel review to help refine and validate the data collection procedures (See Appendix A for interview question validation procedures). Expert panel reviews are considered individuals who are professionals in the field or related to the topic of interest (Hennink et al., 2011). Both experts on the panel held doctorate degrees and had several years of experience. They have both participated in numerous scholarly research endeavors and have several years of experience in university teaching, and in chairing and co-chaired dissertation committees for numerous doctoral degree students.

Credible qualitative interview questions use an open-ended format with other elements to enable the researcher to probe for more qualities. Scholars have further reinforced the effectiveness of open-ended questions and other elements. McNamara(2009) noted question wording should be open-ended, as neutral as possible, and clearlyworded. The validity and reliability of interview questions promote effectiveness in answering the research question. Issues concerning reflexivity, researcher's voice, and confidentiality need to be considered.

The researcher conducted semi-structured in-depth interviews with selected male and female faculty from public universities in the four geographic regions of Nigeria. A semi-structured, open-ended interview method was employed to gather data. Open-ended interview questions are more objective, less leading, and produce an extensive amount of in-depth data through the subjects' own knowledge and feelings. An interview guide involving a few broad and guiding questions was used and supported by probes and prompts (Baumbusch, 2010). This interview form explores the in-depth experiences of research participants and the meanings they attribute to the experiences (Adams, 2010). Good listening skills and emotional control are adopted for effectiveness (Adams, 2010).

The study participants were privy to the interview protocol form, which consisted of the research topic, date of interview, time, location, and the name of the interviewer and the interviewee. The form contained a note to the interviewee thanking him or her for participation and the significance of his or her input in helping the professional practice. The confidentiality of responses was guaranteed, and the appropriate length of the interview and number of questions were highlighted. A total of 10 questions were administered to the participants. The interview questions posed to participants were as follows:

Introductory Questions

Q1: Are you male or female?

Q2: How long have you been working with the university?

Interview Questions

Q3: Take me back through the history in your career as a female or male faculty with a PhD since you have been in this university.

Q4: What personal experiences have increased your awareness of issues involving gender and diversity?

Q5: How would you describe your experiences working with others with different gender than your own?

Q6: How would you describe factors that deprive female or male faculty the opportunity to occupy a management position and hence participate in decision-making, thus gender equality?

Q7: How would you describe the strategy or strategies your university leadership has used to address diversity challenges including the positives and negatives?

Q8: Do you perceive that there is a gender bias in your educational institution, and if so, what do you perceive as the reasons for it?

Q9: What activities or strategies would you implement to ensure that there is gender equality in your institution?

Q10: If there is not gender equality in an institution do you think it would have an effect on organizational effectiveness and, if so, in what way?

In order to enrich the information and enable qualities from the 10 questions to emerge, Socratic follow-up questions, known as probe questions, were conducted intermittently wherever and whenever necessary.

Focus group. The second data collection technique was a focus group. Timony (2006) used focus groups as a method for gathering female faculty perspectives in a qualitative research study on women faculty in higher education, gender equity, and commitment. Consequently, in the current study, a focus group discussion was employed to ascertain the gender diversity of faculty at the senior management level. The group discussion occurred among selected participants in each zone who shared their thoughts and experiences on the research topic of the study in a 45 minute time frame. This time was enough to observe and take notes. The group discussion was not tape-recorded; rather, notes were taken to give insight into the nonverbal cues of the sample participants.

Reflexivity, Researcher's Voice, and Confidentiality. In qualitative inquiry, reflexive practices provide an opportunity for revising questions and even re-framing the research topic as the project unfolds. It is the process of examining both oneself as researcher and the research relationship to expose the researcher's biases and the disclosure of subjectivity (Creswell, 2007). It is characterized by systematically attending to the context of knowledge construction founded in the course of carrying out the research (RECOUP, 2008).

Reflexivity is important for qualitative researchers and encompasses making the research process itself a focus of inquiry, identifying pre-conceptions, and becoming aware of situational dynamics. Hence, it encompasses constant attention to the researcher's perspective, background and influence on the research process and the effects this has on the researcher, which may affect the research (Newbury, 2011). Researchers practice a substantial amount of self-reflection (RECOUP, 2008).

The *voice of the researcher* is another important element in qualitative research. The researcher's voice is pertinent because people carry out all research, individually or collectively, who make numerous choices and decisions before, during, and after carrying out the research (Jackson & Mazzei, 2009). The researcher's voice in most research reports tends to be lost and for the most part readers are unable to recognize it in the research ideas, questions, designs, data collection methods, interpretation, and results. Yet, it is the voice of the researcher that provides an understanding of the concepts in the research. The researcher's voice is a critical response to conventional, interpretive, and critical conceptions of voice in qualitative inquiry.

In qualitative interviewing, maintaining participant confidentiality while presenting valuable, rich, and exhaustive accounts presents distinct challenges (Kaiser, 2009). The research ethics and methods do not sufficiently address these challenges.

Nevertheless, researchers take responsibility and protect their participants through an informed consent process. *Confidentiality* protects the privacy of participants. Researchers are mindful of reporting research results in a way that protects participant confidentiality and disallows retribution.

Although confidentiality allows non-disclosure of information shared with the researcher, some argue that it does protect secrecy, which may inhibit transformative actions. Sound research is a moral and ethical endeavor that is concerned with ensuring that the interests of participants in a study are not harmed as a result of the research.

However, the middle ground allows some type of human subjects review process, allowing participants to grant permission for participation after they have been informed of the possible risks and benefits of the research.

Methodological Assumptions

The research method was qualitative because the goal was to describe, explore, and explain the phenomenon being studied. Consequently, the primary concern of the study was to answer the question of "What factors contribute to the disproportionate representation of female and male faculty at the senior management level in public Nigerian universities?" Such subjective research is the purpose of using a qualitative research design.

Although mixed methods research exists in the middle and integrates the elements of both qualitative and quantitative approaches, significant differences exist between qualitative and quantitative research. However, qualitative and quantitative research methods use passive and active primary forms of data collection.

Data collection methods include primary and secondary data. Secondary data are associated with data collected by others meant for other purposes. This form of data collection tends to save time and effort and is inexpensive. Primary data represent data collected from original sources for a specific purpose. Primary data collection methods are either passive or active. Davis (2000) explained that the passive primary data method encompasses the observation of characteristics by human or non-personal means of the elements under study, while active primary data comprise the questioning of the sampled population by personal and non-personal means.

Chen (2011) explained that the quantitative method measures specific characteristics using structured data collection procedures. This method of research employs large samples of participants because it gives the analysis more statistical power. Creswell (2008) framed quantitative research methods in terms of numbers or quantities and closed-ended questions, and consequently quantitative hypotheses. The results are determined numerically and statistically and variables are tested through various working hypotheses for causes and effects (Chen, 2011).

In contrast, qualitative research is more focused on differences in quality than quantity. It is a process for exploring and understanding the meaning individuals or groups ascribe to a social or human problem (Creswell, 2008). It emphasizes the great and multifaceted complexity characterizing human experience and the socio-cultural context in which humans act (Goussinsky, Reshef, Yanay-Ventura, & Yassour-Borochowitz, 2011).

Qualitative methods are more for exploratory purposes. In addition, fewer sample participants are used because the depth of the data collection does not allow for large numbers of participants. It employs in-depth investigation of an unstructured nature,using a very limited sample, with no attempt made to be representative of the population(Davis, 2000, p. 315). The results are reported using words or pictures rather than numbers. Creswell (2008) framed qualitative research in terms of using words and open-ended questions, and thus qualitative interview questions.

Nevertheless, both the quantitative and qualitative research approaches have key characteristics. While qualitative research collects data on fewer participants and more detail about each participant is known, quantitative research collects data on more participants so it is not possible to have the depth and breadth of knowledge about each. Qualitative data present a depth and richness that may not be possible with the quantitative data. However, because qualitative research is more open to different interpretations, qualitative researchers may be more prone to accusations of bias and personal subjectivity.

Of equal importance, quantitative research includes that statistical analysis allows for generalization (to some extent) to others. Samples closely resemble the population soresults can be projected to the entire population (Davis, 2000, p. 315). It allows researchers to test specific hypotheses. Depending on the research findings, hypotheses are either supported or not supported. Yet, quantitative research methods are not good for studying and analyzing causal relations among social phenomena (Chen, 2011), such as the question used to guide the current study.

Procedures

Data collection occurred through multiple channels using face-to-face interviews and a focus group with sample participants drawn from four public universities in four geographic regions of Nigeria to explore the gender diversity of faculty at the senior management level in public Nigerian universities. Face-to-face interviews and focus groups can be more expensive than telephone or e-mail interviews, but enable the building of trust and rapport with the sample participants and enable the researcher to observe nonverbal interactions. These types of interviews are useful because participants can provide historical information (Creswell, 1998).

The researcher sought access to each of the four public university locations in the four geographic zones of Nigeria to conduct interviews and a focus group. The university locations were Abuja, in the federal capital territory and North-Central zone of Nigeria; Nsukka, in the South-East zone of Nigeria. Otuoke (Bayelsa State) in the South-South zone of Nigeria; and Ibadan, in the South-West zone of Nigeria.

The access procedures used to locate male and female faculty in each university location were similar. None of the universities requested a formal application; rather, each university offered to facilitate access to the faculty. Consequently, access to the male and female faculty in each university location was completed by phoning our contact person at each university location. In Nigeria, telephone communication is easier, speedy, and more efficient than electronic mail or the postal system. The researcher did not have difficulties obtaining access to the male and female faculty because the universities were delighted with the topic of research. The study was approved instantly over the phone and names and telephone numbers of male and female faculty members who met the selection criteria of the study were made available for contact.

The selection criteria for the faculty in the study were female and male faculty who possessed a doctorate degree in their respective fields of academic endeavor and had particular experience. None of the sample participants were from special ethnic groups,institutionalized groups, or protected groups. All sample participants from the four public universities were male and female full-time faculty at the senior management level in public Nigerian universities and were able to discuss gender from their experiences as faculty.

A total of 40 faculty members' names and telephone numbers were made available. A sample size of 40 respondents was desired because qualitative research methods are often concerned with gathering in-depth understanding of a phenomenon (Dworkin, 2012). The researcher conducted initial telephone conversations with the 40 potential participants. Of the 40 recommended faculty member participants, only 20 (i.e.,10 male and 10 female) volunteered to participate in the study. There were five faculty members from each of the selected public universities in the four geographic zones.Table 1 shows the demographics in each selected university.

Table 1.

Participant Demographics

University	Geographic Zone	Female	Male	Total
Abuja University	North-Central	2	3	5
University of Nigeria, Nsukka	South-East	3	2	5
Federal University, Otuoke	South-South	3	2	5
University of Ibadan	South-West	2	3	5
Total		10	10	20

All 20 volunteer participants indicated concern about confidentiality and were guaranteed confidentiality of the information in the final report. The participants were assigned unique identifiers known only to the researcher and given pseudonyms. The confidentiality of the respondents in terms of protecting the written documents was also guaranteed. The participants did not assent to have the interviews recorded through audiotaping and preferred the interviews to be captured only on paper. Their reasoning related to fear of retribution (i.e., they did not want to lose their jobs). The interviews were conducted in a location that was convenient for each faculty member to reduce distractions and interruptions and to ensure privacy.

All Institutional Review Board (IRB) terms were reviewed and all participants knew they were truly volunteers who could withdraw their participation at any time. All data are stored at the home of the researcher in a hidden and locked location to be destroyed upon completion of the project. No written documents were distributed other than the interview questions as part of the interviewing if it became necessary for clarity. All information was treated as highly confidential and protected. The confidentiality of participants' responses was guaranteed. Each of the participants signed the written informed consent form prior to commencing the interview. There were no evident risks and no foreseen or anticipated harm to the participants.

A total of 10 questions were designed for the interviews, and the researcher also used Socratic follow-up (i.e., probing questions) to elicit responses regarding factors that contribute to the disproportionate representation of female and male faculty at the senior management level in public Nigerian universities.

The interview and focus group format offered the researcher the opportunity to meet the female and male faculty at the senior management level in public Nigerian universities and ask for their honest responses to questions related to gender diversity of faculty. The interviews and focus group also helped elicit extensive reports on shared experiences of the female and male faculty at the senior management level in public Nigerian universities. At the end of each interviews and focus group session within, the researcher expressed gratitude to the participants for their time.

The time for the interviews was 45 minutes. The interviews were conducted within a 90-day period at each university in a location that was convenient for each faculty member. The reason for this was to reduce distractions and interruptions and to ensure privacy. The transparency of the research was enhanced by detailed notes taken during the interviews. Additionally, focus group notes were also maintained to give insight into the nonverbal cues of the sample participants and guide against the loss of information.

Because data collection procedures that include in-depth interviews and focus groups are subject to different forms of ethical rigor, the volunteer participants' accounts were taken seriously to ensure that integrity was not compromised. Data collection was anonymous and confidential as detailed in the informed consent release. Participants were informed about the purpose of the research, made to understand the risks they may face as a result of being part of the research, understand the benefits, and allowed to make an independent decision without fear of negative consequences. Participants were given sufficient opportunity to consider whether to participate and the researcher endeavored to avoid coercion and implied overt and covert or undue influence (Argosy University, 2012, p. 25). Participants were protected through the informed consent process. The ethical principles of beneficence, anonymous and justice (Hennink etal., 2011) were used. In order to further guarantee the transparency of the study,intentional deception that would violate participants' rights was avoided.

Data Processing and Analysis

This qualitative research study involved the use of interviews and a focus group to explore the gender diversity of faculty at the senior management level in public universities in Nigeria. The interviews and focus group were the primary source of information.

NVivo software was employed to analyze the information gathered from the interviews with participants in the study. The NVivo software enabled the researcher to open code the narratives, expressions, and terms related to the interview questions. Interview data were coded using open, axial, and selective coding. The coding process involved the creation of nodes for individual emergent themes. Data organization involved organizing nodes into a tree-like hierarchy to demonstrate the prominence of the nodes in the analysis. It was also necessary to emphasize that the tree nodes were identified as NVivo identified consistency in relation to percentages of occurrence.

The process of coding information into open coding, axial coding, and selective coding occurred in stages. Open coding was the first stage and involved a process of breaking down, examining, comparing, conceptualizing, and categorizing data. It is the"initial stage for coding the data for its major categories" (Creswell, 1998, p. 64). Axial coding was the second stage and involved reassembling the data to allow for the exploration and discovery of possible relationships, patterns, and emerging themes (Hennink et al., 2011). Selective coding was the final stage. In this stage the core category was systematically related to other categories to validate relationships and expand categories that needed further refinement and development.

Tree nodes were used to identify various open coding premises or common responses most commonly used to complete the axial coding process. The NVivo software identifies individual participant responses that are most consistent with the selective coding composite response and links them to the tree and free nodes of interest for the interview question (Hennink et al., 2011). The completion of the stages of the data analysis of all interview questions associated with the research question led to the generation of themes to characterize the responses to each question.

Analysis of the Investigation in the Context of Validity or Reliability. In the study, analyzing participants' responses allowed for triangulation of themes that commonly occurred (Dees, 2010). The related processes of triangulation, crystallization, and saturation are often applied to generate a theme. The data were triangulated with interviews and a focus group.

Triangulation. The researcher used methodological triangulation that included interviews and observations to check and establish validity in this research study by analyzing the research question from multiple perspectives. Evidence was collaborated from different sources in order to shed light on a perspective (Creswell, 2007).

Integrity. Integrity underpins ethical practice in all the activities that comprise data collection and analysis (Watts, 2008). There is an awareness that all forms of data collection are subject to some form of ethical rigor. In-depth interviews, participant observation, and non-participant observation may entail different forms of ethical rigor in their execution. Therefore, the participants' accounts were taken seriously to ensure integrity was not compromised.

Trustworthiness. In qualitative research, trustworthiness supports the fact that the research findings are worth paying attention to. In qualitative research, issues of trustworthiness demand attention to credibility, transferability, dependability, and confirmability. It is different from the conventional experimental precedent of attempting to show validity, soundness, and significance.

Transferability. Transferability is the generalization of the study findings to other situations and contexts. Transferability is not considered a viable naturalistic research objective. Therefore, the researcher supplied a highly detailed description of the research situation and methods. Transferability is most relevant to qualitative research methods, particularly in ethnography and case studies.

Summary

This chapter provided the theoretical foundation and methods used to explore the gender diversity of male and female faculty at the senior management level in public Nigerian universities. The chapter enabled the understanding of the factors that contribute to the disproportionate representation of female and male faculty at the senior management level in public Nigerian universities.

A total of 20 participants volunteered to participate in the study, 10 male and 10 female faculty members at the senior management level in public Nigerian universities. All participants indicated concern about confidentiality and were guaranteed confidentiality of the information in the final report. The participants were assigned unique identifiers known only to the researcher and given pseudonyms. All IRB terms were reviewed and all participants knew they were truly volunteers who could withdraw their participation at any time.

Interview and focus group discussions were conducted with male and female faculty in each selected public university from the four geographic zones. A total of 10 questions were designed for the interviews, and the researcher also used Socratic follow-up (i.e., probing questions) to elicit responses regarding factors that contribute to the disproportionate representation of female and male faculty at the senior management level in public Nigerian universities. The time for the interviews was 45 minutes. The interviews were conducted within a 90-day period at each university in a location that was convenient for each faculty member. The reason for this was to reduce distractions and interruptions and to ensure privacy. Detailed notes taken during the interviews and focus group notes to give insight into the nonverbal cues of the sample participants and guide against the loss of information enhanced the transparency of the research.

The researcher employed the NVivo software to analyze the information gathered from the interviews and focus group. NVivo allowed the researcher to open code the narratives, expressions, and terms related to the interview questions. The coding process occurred in stages and reflected the sequence of open coding, axial coding, and selective coding. The completion of the stages of the data analysis led to the generation of themes to characterize the responses to each question.

The decision to study gender diversity and gain an understanding of the factors that contribute to the disproportionate representation of female and male faculty at the senior management level in public Nigerian universities was effective for this study because of the uniqueness of the study to public Nigerian universities. Missing from the study was the perceptions of faculty from private Nigerian universities, which would have enriched the results. The approach to this investigation was suitable for exploring gender diversity in public Nigerian universities, accommodating the qualitative data essential for assessing factors that contribute to the disproportionate representation of female and male faculty at the senior management level in public Nigerian universities.

‖‖‖

CHAPTER FIVE

RESULTS OF THE INVESTIGATION

The investigation was very informative. Face-to-face interviews and a focus group were conducted to capture and code participants' responses to the interview questions, triangulate nonverbal body language with verbal responses, and ensure the integrity of data. The open, axial, and selective coding data analysis procedures related to the interview question responses were used to explain the gathered information. Data were collected and the themes that emerged are evaluated and described in this chapter.

As previously stated, the purpose of this investigation was to explore the gender diversity of faculty at the senior management level in public Nigerian universities. The research involved the use of a qualitative descriptive approach to seek the perceptions of gender disparity held by faculty at the senior management level in public Nigerian universities. Data were collected through in-depth interviews and a focus group and managed with NVivo software. Male and female faculty at the senior management level in public Nigerian universities were interviewed to understand what factors contribute to the disproportionate representation of female and male faculty at the senior management level in public Nigerian universities.

Results

The first two questions were introductory questions meant to familiarize the researcher with the participants and at the same time shape the pattern of the interview. Therefore, the first two questions are highlighted in the form of reports, rather than interview answers. Interview questions 3 through 10 were used to probe participants on issues associated with the research question, seeking their perception of what factors contribute to the disproportionate representation of female and male faculty at the senior management level in public Nigerian universities.

Introductory Questions

Question 1. Are you male or female?

Equal numbers of male and female faculty members were interviewed. Instead of 20 male and 20 female faculty members totaling 40 participants as previously planned, the researcher was able to interview 10 male and 10 female faculty members, for a total sample of 20 faculty members at the senior management level in public Nigerian universities across the four geographic zones.

Question 2. How long have you been working with the university?

Most participants had been working in public Nigerian universities for between 3 and 15 years. The researcher carefully chose this participant group to honor the changes resulting so far from globalization in these public universities.

Interview Questions

Question 3. Take me back through the history in your career as a female or male faculty with a Ph.D. since you have been in this university.

(Juliet) As a female, I feel like there has not been an equitable distribution of power or position in the university. In my university in the senior management position, we have three female faculties and 11 male faculties. Similarly, in the Senate, we have five female faculties and 11 male faculties.

(Catherine) You may want to know that the Senate is the governing body of the university and all university decisions that include student result approvals, staff and faculty promotions are made, then, where are we now if we do not have representation.

(Rose) The male faculty head committees in the university as department chairs in the Senate, though as a female faculty, I may say that I feel good working in the university; but all position areas of the university are mostly open to the male faculties because of cultural issues. For example, the male faculties are more disposed to travelling and attending workshops. The female faculties are not usually confident and disposed to take such trips because of culture bias.

(Joseph) From the male faculty perspective, I feel I have more opportunities here in this university as a male faculty. I have headed and serve in various committees.

(George) I feel bold to say that though my female faculty counterpart has similar opportunities, it is not the same with that of their male counterpart because in most part, this opportunity depends on capacity.

Question 4. What personal experiences have increased your awareness of issues involving gender and diversity?

(Mary) I think substantial disparity exists between male and female faculty in our universities. The disparity is in the number of female and male faculty. Generally speaking, in the context of the university as a whole, male faculty significantly outnumber their female counterpart[s].

Socratic Follow-up Question 4a. Do you have an idea what the ratio or number would be?

(Mary) As a female faculty in the university, I think the ratio of disparity is about one female faculty to about 10 male faculties.

(Philip) I do not think that the given ratio is correct; I think the disparity ratio of male and female faculties stands at 60:40 (male faculty at 60% and female 40%).

(Ken) If I may add, in our universities, the disparity in the number of female makes it difficult to find female faculty representation in the university's governing council, the highest decision-making body. Because all representation in the university's governing council is by election and the female faculty is in the minority, making their representation farfetched.

*(Robert)*As a follow up to the last speaker, I accept, there is also disparity between female and male faculties in the senior management position as Deans, head of department, and registrar. In my opinion, I can say that this disparity is also attributable to culture, skill, and capacity. These factors are responsible for the low female and high male faculty ratio in the university.

(Doris) No matter what is been said, in our university, the male faculties have more opportunity than their female faculties counterpart.

Socratic Follow-up Question 4b. Please can you tell me more about how women and men faculty perceive themselves?

(Mary) From the female perspectives, I see the distinction between male and female faculty very vividly in employments and appointments. Employment and appointments [are] more open to the male faculty than their female counterpart.This has impacted and increased my awareness of gender diversity.

(Doris) Much more attention are given to male faculty, they are just more visible than their female counterpart. But for the female faculty, to be noticed you have to make yourself visible, whereas the male faculties are already visible.

(Robert) From the male perspective, I think that significant distinction exists between us male faculty and the female faculty. Naturally, this distinction tends to favor us the male faculties because it is promoted by culture and stimulates stereotyping against women.

Question 5. How would you describe your experiences working with others with different gender than your own?

(Angela) In general terms, the relationship between male and female faculties is somehow cordial.

Socratic Follow-up Question 5a. You used the word "somehow," please can you give me some example of different experiences between men and women?

(Angela) As a female faculty, the male faculties are egoistic, prompting domineering attitudes over us their female counterpart. They look down on female[s] and do not mind ideas originating from female[s] nor respect our voices.

(Andrew) As a male faculty, I think that the female faculties' population is very small when compared to us their male counterpart because women do not apply for university jobs. Besides, women believe that the men are domineering, but I do not think it is really the case. Going from the African culture men occupy the position of head of the family.

Question 6. How would you describe factors that deprive female or male faculty the opportunity to occupy management position and hence participate in decision-making, thus gender equality?

(Timothy) To be very candid and honest, I think culture bias inhibits women from occupying management position in the universities. Culture bias manifests in different ways, stimulating and promoting prejudice, stereotyping and even ethnicity. Our culture does not see women at the forefront, rather sees women ['s] position and place in the domestic setting, thus at home rather than in corporations or universities as decision-makers. As a result, there are fewer educated women to take up management position.

Socratic Follow-up Question 6a. Please can you tell me more about factors like prejudice, stereotyping, ethnicity and other issues you might know?

(Timothy) Women are usually seen as more emotional than rational and [an] assumption exists that they may not perform well. The progress of a single mother in the department is always at a slow pace compared to her male counterpart. Of equal importance, depending on the zone, culture and customs differ significantly. A female and a Christian may find it difficult to work with comfort if hired in a Muslim male-dominated university setting.

(Paulina) Let me add also that depending on the zone, culture and customs may differ significantly and further stimulate cultural bias, such that women faculty population in such zone may even be lower. Consequently, such that in the social sphere women perceived bias promoted by the existing culture stimulates and promotes prejudice, stereotyping, and ethnicity.

Question 7. How would you describe the strategy or strategies your university leadership has used to address diversity challenges including the positives and negatives?

(Paul) I think now in the hiring process leadership tries to be sensitive to gender diversity. Consideration is given to some women applicants to avoid lopsided hiring of men. Women are encouraged to participate and in most part, deliberate appointments are given to women.

Socratic Follow-up Question 7a. Please can you give me some example of strategy or strategies your university uses in addressing diversity challenges?

(Paul) Today, I think that universities are beginning to follow the Nigeria federal government guideline for hiring. The federal government advocates job adverts requesting that women apply. Gender diversity is sensitized during hiring. Female faculty applicants are hired to avoid lopsided hiring male faculty. Equal employment opportunity is advocated. In most cases they use the slogan "women are encouraged to apply." Brilliant undergraduate women are encouraged pursuing postgraduate studies and guaranteed job after the postgraduate studies in the university. Consequently, in my opinion, this proper mobilization of women to step up in decision-making has increased more women participation in recent times.

(Paulina) But the issue is that when female faculty are employed, if the female faculty want to be listened to, she has about phrasing her line of reasoning in a some way more male to be accepted.

Question 8. Do you perceive that there is a gender bias in your educational institution and, if so, what do you perceive as the reasons for it?

(John) I think there is no gender bias at the academic level in the educational institution because the demand for hiring is based on qualification and discipline of study.

(Theresa) I disagree because on the social sphere, I think some form of bias exists, and usually promoted by the existing culture in the form of prejudice, stereotyping, and ethnicity. This opinion may not actually portray the reasoning of all the genders. Most male faculty believes and thinks that there is no bias whatsoever.

(Bridget) Also in our culture, you must agree with me that for women there is a need to prove yourself and their men counterpart are perceived as having more knowledge than women.

Question 9. What activities or strategies would you implement to ensure that there is gender equality in your institution?

(Bridget) I think as female faculties one of the strategies would be to advertise the hiring position to enable men and women applicants the opportunity to apply for the job.In addition, hiring applications should be separated by gender, bringing all qualified applicants and choosing from men and women. The employment process should be seen to bridge the gap between men and women through the equal opportunity employment strategy.

(Raymond) Though I agree with Bridget, but as a male faculty, I think that may not be the solution to male and female equality in our universities. Now in here, I think that culture sees the men as being superior; there is lack of mobilization on the part of the women. Therefore, proper mobilization of women to step up in decision making may increase women ['s] participation. Suggestively also, to enhance knowledge on diversity and begin to bridge the diversity gap between men and women, I think mandatory seminars and workshops as well as public enlightenment for both men and women to attend may be the way to enhance knowledge on diversity and bridge the diversity gap between men and women.

(Agnes) Also in our university much attention should be paid to gender studies. There is need to teach our children on the importance of gender equality at an early beginning. This will help eradicate prejudice, stereotyping, and ethnicity in the nearest future.

Question 10. If there is no gender equality in an institution, do you think it would have an effect on organizational effectiveness and, if so, in what way?

(Catherine) As female, I think that no gender equality in our institutions would definitely affect organizational effectiveness. The lack of gender equality will inhibit some useful ideas from women that could grow the university. Women exclusion in decision-making may discourage women inputs and presentation of such useful idea of growth as well. In the right frame work, ideas must be seen as an idea coming from the right of objectivity, be it male or female idea.

(Ken) As male faculty, I see this very differently. I am not really concerned with gender equality or diversity as the case may be, but as a male faculty, I advocate "competition" as a necessary tool to actively stimulate organizational effectiveness. I think it is the proper necessary tool. As a male faculty, I am all out for the best should be selected whether male or female.

Socratic Follow-up Question 10a. Please can you tell me in detail more about your organizational culture as it pertains to professional development workshop for faculty on diversity?

(Mary) Though equal employment opportunity is advocated, however, on campuses, there is no awareness on professional development workshop within the respective universities for faculties on diversity in most part. (Catherine) I think there is always hypocrisy paid to diversity by the administration. This really bothers me and it is a problem, but I still like it in my university.

Open Coding

Based on the open coding, the highlights indicated five categories: gender inequality, factor constraints, gender relations, factors promoting diversity, and gender opinion.

Gender Inequality

Gender inequality refers to the disparity associated with male faculty significantly outnumbering female faculty, thus contributing to the disproportionate representation of female and male faculty at the senior management level in public Nigerian universities.This disparity has led to a lack of an equitable distribution of power or position in the university, with male faculty occupying a greater number of positions of power. The themes gathered from the discussions for questions 3 and 4 cited the inequalities.

- Substantial disparity exists between male and female faculty in our universities.

- Male faculty significantly outnumbers their female counterpart[s]. Female faculties think the ratio of disparity is about one female faculty to about 10 male faculties.

- Male faculty's counterpart associates the disparity ratio of male and female faculties at 60:40 (male faculty at 60% and female 40%).

Factor Constraints

Factor constraints are constraints that impede or inhibit female faculty at the senior management level in public Nigerian universities from occupying senior management positions and experiencing better opportunities. Such constraints are associated with culture bias that manifests in the form of prejudice, stereotyping, and ethnicity, and significantly contribute to the disproportionate representation of female and male faculty at the senior management level in public Nigerian universities. The themes for questions 3, 4, 5, 6, and 8 highlight specifically the factor constraints.

- There is disparity between female and male faculties in the senior management position as Deans, head of department, and registrar.

- All position areas of the university are mostly open to the male faculties because of cultural issues.

- Male faculty has more opportunities.

- This disparity is also attributable to culture, skill, and capacity.

- The disparity in the number of female makes it difficult to find female faculty representation in the university's governing council, the highest decision making body.

- Representation in the university's governing council is by election and the female faculty is in the minority, making their representation farfetched.

- The distinction between male and female faculty is very vividly in employments and appointments.

- This distinction tends to favor the male faculties because it is promoted by culture and stimulates stereotyping against women.

- Culture bias inhibits women from occupying management position.

- Culture bias manifests in different ways, stimulating and promoting prejudice, stereotyping, and even ethnicity.

- Culture sees women ['s] position and place in the domestic setting, thus at home rather than in corporations or universities as decision-makers.

- Women are usually seen as more emotional than rational and [an] assumption exists that they may not perform well.

- A female and a Christian may find it difficult to work with comfort if hired in a Muslim male-dominated university setting.

- Depending on the zone, culture and customs may differ significantly and further stimulate cultural bias, such that women faculty population in such zone may even be lower.

- Female faculties' population is very small because women do not apply for university jobs.

- There are fewer educated women to take up management position.

- The progress of a single mother in the department is always at a slow pace compared to her single father counterpart.

- On the social sphere, some form of bias exists, and promoted by the existing culture in the form of prejudice, stereotyping, and ethnicity.

Gender Relations

Gender relations emphasize male and female faculty relations at the senior management level in public Nigerian universities. Though relationships between male and female faculties tend to be cordial at the senior management level, such relationships are still influenced by the African culture. The African cultural orientation asserts men take the position of head of the family. As a result, male faculty tends to have domineering attitudes over their female counterparts. Women are undervalued, thus contributing to the disproportionate representation of female and male faculty in the senior management level in public

Nigerian universities. The theme for questions 5 and 8 highlighted gender relations.

- Relationship between male and female faculties is somehow cordial.

- Male faculties are egoistic, prompting domineering attitudes over us their female counterpart.

- Look down on female[s] and do not mind ideas originating from female[s] nor respect our voices.

- Going from the African culture men occupy the position of head of the family.

- There is no gender bias at the academic level in the educational institution because the demand for hiring is based on qualification and discipline of study.

- Most male faculty believes and thinks that there is no bias whatsoever.

Factors Promoting Diversity

Factors promoting diversity include different ranges of instruments and stimuli that are used to promote diversity within public Nigerian universities. Such instruments and stimuli were highlighted in open coding, but do not play a significant role in gender equality in public Nigerian universities. The evidence from this study suggests that gender inequality persist in public Nigerian universities and highlights prejudice, stereotyping, and cultural bias as primary inhibiting factors that contribute to the disproportionate representation of female and male faculty at the senior management level. Loden and Rosener (1991) also corroborated these factors in their study. The theme for questions 7 and 9 was factors promoting diversity.

- The federal government advocates job adverts requesting that women apply.

- Gender diversity is sensitized during hiring.

- Female faculty applicants are hired to avoid lopsided hiring male faculty.

- Women are encouraged to participate and in most part, deliberate appointments are given to women.

- Equal employment opportunity is advocated.

- Brilliant undergraduate women are encouraged pursuing postgraduate studies and guaranteed job after the postgraduate studies in the university.

- Proper mobilization of women to step up in decision-making has increased more women participation in recent times.

- Advertise the hiring position to enable men and women applicants the opportunity to apply for the job.

- Hiring applications should be separated by gender, bringing all qualified applicants and choosing from men and women.

- The employment process should be seen to bridge the gap between men and women through the equal opportunity employment strategy.

- Proper mobilization of women to step up in decision-making may increase women participation.

- Mandatory seminars and workshops as well as public enlightenment for both men and women to attend may be the way to enhance knowledge on diversity and bridge the diversity gap between men and women.

Gender Opinion

Gender opinion reflects the opinions of the female and male faculty members who were interviewed. It was not surprising that there were divergent opinions among the genders. The female faculty members predominantly emphasized the need for professional development workshops within their respective universities to promote diversity, while the male faculty members advocated competition as a necessary tool to stimulate and promote organizational effectiveness. However, the request that female faculty apply for a senior management position and deliberate appointments given to women may genuinely contribute to gender equality and better bridge the diversity gap between male and female faculty. The gender opinions were highlighted in the theme for question 10 denoted as gender relations.

- No gender equality in the institutions would affect organizational effectiveness.

- The lack of gender equality will inhibited some useful ideas from women that could grow the university.

- Women['s] exclusion in decision-making may discourage women['s] inputs and presentation of such useful idea of growth.

- Ideas must be seen as an idea coming from the right of objectivity, be it male or female idea.

- As male faculty, I am not really concerned with gender equality.

- Male faculty advocate "competition" as a necessary tool to actively stimulate organizational effectiveness. The best should be selected whether male or female.

- On campuses, there is no awareness on professional development workshop within the respective universities for faculties on diversity.

Axial Coding

Axial coding looks at the frequency of open coding categories. The NVivo assisted axial coding revealed the themes associated with the problem of gender diversity at the senior management level in public Nigerian universities were gender inequality and factor constraints.

The theme emphasized gender inequality as a reflection of gender disparity associated with male faculty significantly outnumbering female faculty. From the female gender perspective, the ratio was 1:10 in favor of male faculty, while from the male perspective the ratio was 60:40 in favor of male faculty. Consequently, there are more male faculty than female faculty in public Nigerian universities. This disparity in the ratio has inhibited female representation in the university governing council, the highest decision-making body that is usually by election as well as makes it difficult to find female faculty in senior management positions.

The factor constraints exposed as culture bias also manifested in the form of prejudice, stereotyping, and ethnicity and remained an inhibiting factor in female faculty occupying senior management positions. For the most part, the culture views men as being superior, making female faculty perceive their male faculty counterparts as egoistic and domineering. Female faculty are perceived as emotional rather than rational, leading to the assumption that female faculty may not perform as well as their male counterparts, promoting the lack of mobilization on the part of the women. The culture sees women's position as in the domestic setting at home rather than in corporations or universities as decision-makers. As a result, there are fewer educated women to take management positions. This perception excludes women from decision-making and participation in senior management positions, thereby discouraging women's input and presentation of useful idea of growth.

There was insufficient evidence to collaborate that the universities employ from time to time on-campus professional development strategies for faculty to correct the imbalance related to the slow progress of females (single or married) compared to their male counterparts. Professional development on-campus tools such as mandatory seminars, workshops for faculty on diversity, and public enlightenment for both men and women are necessary to strengthen organizational effectiveness. Male faculty are not really concerned with gender equality; rather, they advocate for "competition" as a necessary tool to actively stimulate organizational effectiveness.

Such a mindset may be counterproductive. Instead, employment processes should bridge the gap between men and women through the equal opportunity employment strategy. Perhaps gender equality in the employment process should be made a rule within the university policy rather than competition. This process will enable female faculty members to occupy management positions in the same number as their male counterparts and significantly reduce male faculty members outnumbering female faculty members in most public Nigerian universities. The distinction between male and female faculty is vivid in employments and appointments. It may be adequate that universities regularly embrace their commitment to diversity in mission statements, strategic plans, websites, and marketing materials (Figueroa, 2012).

Selective Coding

The selective coding composite responses as defined by the thematic relationships were denoted as a "disproportionate representations of female and male faculty in the senior management level is a problem in public Nigerian universities" because there is pronounced gender inequality and evidence of several factor constraints.

Summary

The participants in this study were very helpful in providing rich and thick feedback to enhance the results of the investigation. While the male faculty may have had a little less concern for the disparity of the situation, they still spoke very openly about their perceptions. Of course, because there are more male faculty in these universities they did not feel a threat to their positions by their female counterparts. Because of this disparity in numbers, leadership is going to have to shoulder the responsibility of trying to resolve this for the good of the whole. From the interviews, it is obvious that for the country to move forward and benefit from the wealth of talent that includes female educator, leadership will have to play greater role in moving equality forward.

CHAPTER SIX

INVESTIGATORY PERCEPTIONS

Discussion

Though several studies revealed the importance of gender diversity in both organizations and educational institutions, no substantial evidence exists supporting its integration into public Nigerian universities. The ways in which diversity is promoted in public Nigerian universities are still evolving and no exhaustive explanations have been reached surrounding the gender disparity of faculty at the senior management level. Therefore, there was a need to explore the gender diversity of faculty at the senior management level in public Nigerian universities. The research question used to guide the current study was "What factors contribute to the disproportionate representation of female and male faculty at the senior management level in public Nigerian universities?"

The theoretical analysis of the gender diversity of faculty at the senior management level in public Nigerian universities could not be accomplished and completed without defining diversity, exposing the role of culture in diversity, uncovering the process of managing gender diversity, and exploring the role of leadershipin diversity. The complexity inherent in the concept of diversity has stimulated severaldefinitions and supports the enormous challenge of managing diversity in educational institutions. Nevertheless, the definitions provided by Bukhari and Sharma (2014), the American Management Association (2014), Kapoor (2011), Hur et al. (2010), Meisterand Willyerd (2010), Daft (2007),

Kim (2006), Rijamampianina and Carmichael (2005),Van Es (2003), Gardenswartz and Rowe (2003), and Pajares and Valiante (2001) support evidence to reach the conclusion that diversity reflects differences stimulated by how employees perceive their workplace and the disparity associated with demographic elements that pose potential barriers to the organization. This element of disparity leads to challenges, but when managed effectively, can provide a strategic advantage to public Nigerian universities.

Of equal importance, the culture role in diversity represents a predominant factor of interest in the study into why gender disparity exists in Nigerian universities. This is because the cultural composition of the collectivistic countries of sub-Sahara Africa, including Nigeria, lean toward masculine traits and expose women as the weaker gender.Such culture induced gender bias in the form of prejudice and stereotyping is among the root causes of gender disparity among male and female faculty in public Nigerian universities. This view is also supported by Ayub et al. (2013), Rai (2012), and Gathers(2003).

The process of managing diversity involves creating value from human differences and similarities. Such differences and similarities encompass values and motivate individual employees in a diverse setting to work as a team. Diversity can be better managed through a workplace management system designed to stimulate employment equity programs. Accordingly, the characteristic of effective diversity management is associated with leadership patterns and styles. The leadership competence of diversity management depends on the leadership strategy encompassing a variety of initiatives that enhance organizational performance. The leadership style and levels of communication, team building, and motivation influence such initiatives. A stronger leadership role may address and resolve diverse workforce issues because a formidable association exists between leadership and diversity. Similarly,leadership role can help decrease the challenges that affect how public Nigerian universities recruit employees, communicate, and motivate a diverse workgroup.Integrating employment equity, affirmative action, and diversity management can enable diversity to become an asset in public Nigerian universities.

The current study was guided by a qualitative descriptive approach to explore the gender disparity of faculty at the senior management level in public Nigerian universities. The sample participants were male and female faculty at the senior management level in public Nigerian universities drawn on site from four public universities in the four geographic zones of Nigeria: North-Central, South-South, South-East, and South-West. The data collection occurred through face-to-face interviews and a focus group becausethey enabled the researcher to build trust and rapport with the sample participants and exposed the nonverbal cues given by the participants. The interviews and focus group captured the perceptions of male and female faculty in Nigerian public universities.

Summary

The research question used to guide the investigation was "What factors contribute to the disproportionate representation of female and male faculty at the senior management level in public Nigerian universities?" A small sample size of 20 participants volunteered for the investigation. Participants included male and female faculty members who had particular experience and possessed a doctorate degree in their respective fields of academic endeavor. Interviews and a focus group were used to answer the qualitative research question. The interviews and focus group included an informal, conversational, general interview guide approach and Socratic follow-up interview questions. For the most part, the questions and discussions shed light on the ways in which female and male faculty relate in public Nigerian universities as well as gender diversity at the senior management level.

All interviews and the focus group took place in a location that was convenient for the faculty members at each selected university in the four geographic zones of Nigeria to guide against distractions and interruptions. The interviews were 45 minutes in length and the data collection period was 3 months. The transparency of the research was enhanced by detailed notes taken during the interviews and focus group to give insight into the nonverbal cues of the sample participants and guide against the loss of information. The researcher used the NVivo software to analyze the information because it enables the open coding of narratives, expressions, and terms related to the interview questions.

The data gathered from the interviews and focus group related to the gender diversity of faculty at the senior management level in public Nigerian universities and was coded using open, axial, and selective coding in stages. Open coding was used to break down, examine, and compare themes and revealed five categories: gender inequality, gender discontent, gender relationships, factor constraints, and factors promoting diversity. Axial coding reassembles the data, allowing for the exploration and discovery of possible relationships, patterns, or emerging themes (Hennink et al., 2011). NVivo assisted the researcher with axial coding, which revealed the themes associated with the problem of gender diversity at the senior management level in public Nigerianuniversities as gender inequality and factor constraints. Selective coding reveal evidence of pronounced gender inequality as well as several factor constraints.

Limitations

As with all other research studies, this study had a few limitations. First, because the nature of the research was exploratory based on perceptions and tailored to the needs of one population, it was difficult to extrapolate findings to more broad populations or draw general or far-reaching conclusions; thus, the outcome of this research depended mostly on the researcher's knowledge and interpretation. Second, the study involved challenges in terms of validity, generalizable results,wider implications, and reliability, reflecting a few limitations that related to the analysis of the interview data. This limitation included the possibility that the researcher's subjective opinions biased the information presented or the conclusions drawn, the ability to generalize results to other populations, and the ability to make broad and sweeping recommendations based on the outcomes of the study.

Nevertheless, the significance of the study relates to the quality of the sample demographics, as the sample participants were male and female full-time faculty members with a doctorate degree in their respective fields of academic endeavor. The sample participants were educated and gave appropriate answers during the interviews, thereby increasing the reliability of the study.

Conclusion

In a broad sense, the findings of the investigation indicate the existence of a pronounced level of gender inequality and several factor constraints among female and male faculty members at the senior management level in public Nigerian universities. The following are recommendations the leadership can implement to try and help promote and enhance diversity and inclusiveness in public Nigerian universities.

First, the information gathered from exploring the gender diversity of faculty at the senior management level in public Nigerian universities can assist leaders in identifying the reasons for the discrepancies. This information can assist leaders in pinpointing the exact reasons for these discrepancies so that they can identify the specifics. By identifying the specifics, less time and resources will be wasted and actions for resolving the problems be implemented very quickly.

Second, the information gathered from the study can assist leaders of public Nigerian universities in identifying effective strategies to eliminate the gender discrepancies within their universities. Such strategies as providing diversity training on campus, as well as developing and implementing an equal opportunity employment policy among genders can be accomplished.

The third recommendation is to use the information gathered in this study to assist the management of public Nigerian universities in thinking about creating committees to amend their mission statements to reflect diversity and equality. University leaders can also implement new policies, such as a more transparent recruitment process and some form of gender equity in personnel policies.

While this investigation was just a snapshot of diversity of gender in Nigeria, we are well aware that this form of disparity exists in so many other countries and organizations around the world. If leaders were willing to understand the importance of diversity to the overall success of their country or organization then they would be able to end the disparity in numbers between genders and their abilities for achievement. Two of the most important benefits from accepting diversity are the amount of innovation it can create and the amount of synergy it can create when individuals are willing to work together because they believe that they will receive fair treatment regardless of gender. A major benefit of this is that embracing diversity can make a country or organization stronger.

REFERENCES

Adams, E. (2010). The joys and challenges of semi-structured interviewing. *Community Practitioner, 83*(7), 18-21.

Ambe-Uva, T. N., Iwuchukwu, O., & Jibrin, L. J. (2008). Gender analysis in National Open University of Nigeria: Implications and policy issues in bridging the divide. *Journal of Applied Sciences Research, 4*(7), 814-825.

American Psychological Association. (2011). *Publication manual of the American Psychological Association* (6th ed.). Washington, DC: Author.

American Management Association. (2014, November 6). *Leading the four generations at work*. Retrieved from http://www.amanet.org/training/articles/Leading-the-Four-Generations-at-Work.aspx

Argosy University.(2012). *Institutional Review Board handbook*. Sarasota, FL: Author.Armstrong, J. (2003, March 24). *Power and prejudice: Some definitions for discussion and analysis*. Retrieved from http://www.unm.edu/~jka/courses/archive/power.html

Ayub, A., Aslam, M. S., Razzaq, A., Iftekhar, H., &Hafeez, S. (2013). Examining factors affecting diversity in the workplace.*Interdisciplinary Journal of Contemporary Research in Business, 4*(12), 642-648.

Bakotié, D. (2008). Leadership styles' specifics in large Croatian companies. The Business Review, Cambridge, 10(2), 213-220.

Baumbusch, J. (2010). Semi-structured interviewing in practice-close research. *Journal for Specialists in Pediatric Nursing, 15*(3), 255-258.

Benson, J. D. (2015). Leadership and motivation. Research *Starters: Business (Online Edition).*

Brown, G. K. (2010). Conceptualizing and measuring ethnicity. *Oxford Development Studies, 38*, 4.

Bukhari, S. S., & Sharma, B. C. (2014).Workplace gender diversity and inclusive growth in public and private organizations. *Indian Journal of Industrial Relations, 49*(3),551.

Cann, A., & Siegfried, W. D. (1990). Gender stereotypes and dimensions of effective leader behavior. *Sex Roles, 23*(7-8), 413.

Carrell, M. R., Mann, E. E., & Sigler, T. H. (2006).Defining workforce diversity programs and practices in organizations: A longitudinal study. *Labor Law Journal, 57*(1), 5-12.

Chen, C. (2011). Quantitative methodology: Appropriate use in research for blind baseball ergonomics and safety design. *The Journal of Human Resource and Adult Learning, 7*(1), 1-6.

Chiu, C., & Hong, Y. (2007). Cultural processes: Basic principles. In A. W. Kruglanski, & E. T. Higgins (Eds.), *Social psychology: Hand-book of basic principles* (pp.785-806). New York, NY: The Guilford Press.

Choi, S., & Rainey, H. G. (2010, January/February). Managing diversity in U.S. federal agencies: Effects of diversity and diversity management on employee perceptions of organizational performance. *Public Administration Review, 70*(1), 109-121.

Churchman, S., & Thompson, C. (2008). Delivering gender diversity: Beyond the business case. *Strategic HR Review, 7*(5), 17-22. doi:10.1108/14754390810893053

Collins, J. (2001). *Good to great*. New York, NY: Harper Business.

Creswell, J. W. (1998). *Qualitative inquiry & research design: Choosing among five traditions*. Thousand Oaks, CA: Sage Publications.

Creswell, J. W. (2007). *Qualitative inquiry and research design: Choosing among five approaches* (2nd ed.). Thousand Oaks, CA: Sage Publications.

Creswell, J. W. (2008). *Research design: Qualitative, quantitative, and mixed methods approaches* (3rd ed.). Thousand Oaks, CA: Sage Publications.

Crouch, M. A. (2012). Implicit bias and gender (and other sorts of) diversity in philosophy and the academy in the context of the corporatized university. *Journal of Social Philosophy, 43*(3), 212-226.

Daft, R. L. (2007). *The leadership experience* (4th ed.). Mason, OH: South-WesternPublishing Company.

Daneci-Patrau, D. (2011). Formal communication in organisation. *Economics, Management and Financial Markets, 6*(1), 487-497.

Davis, D. (2000). *Business research for decision making* (5th ed.). Pacific Grove, CA:Duxbury.

Dees, S. J. R. A. (2010). *A qualitative study of the perceptions of the use of the teacher work sample methodology in student teaching* (Doctoral dissertation). Retrieved from ProQuest Dissertations and Theses database. (3488922)

Deloris, M. W. (2003). Federally regulated corporate communication: An analysis of dominant values.*Corporate Communications, 8*(3), 163-172.

Díaz-García, C., González-Moreno, A., & Sáez-Martínez, F. J. (2013). Gender diversity within R&D teams: Its impact on radicalness of innovation. *Innovation:Management, Policy & Practice, 15*(2), 149-160.

Diekman, A. B., Goodfriend, W., & Goodwin, S. (2004). Dynamic stereotypes of power: Perceived change and stability in gender hierarchies. *Sex Roles, 50*(3-4), 201-215.doi:10.1023/B:SERS.0000015552.22775.44

Dworkin, S. L. (2012). Sample size policy for qualitative studies using in-depth interviews. *Archives of Sexual Behavior, 41*(6), 1319-1320. doi:10.1007/s10508-012-0016-6

Eagly, A. H., Makhijani, M. G., & Klonsky, B. G. (1992, January). Gender and the valuation of leaders: A meta-analysis. *Psychological Bulletin, 111*(1), 3-22.

Essien, A. M., & Ukpong, D. P. (2012). Patriarchy and gender inequality: The persistence of religious and cultural prejudice in contemporary Akwa Ibom State, Nigeria. *International Journal of Social Science and Humanity, 2*(4), 286.doi:10.7763/IJSSH.2012.V2.111

Fang, L. C., & Saini, D. S. (2012). Managing diversity in Chinese and Indian organizations: A qualitative study. *Journal of Chinese Human Resources Management, 3*(1), 16-32. doi:10.1108/20408001211220548

Figueroa, I. (2012). *The role of the Chief Diversity Officer in higher education: A qualitative study of two private universities* (Doctoral dissertation). Retrieved from ProQuest Dissertations and Theses database. (3535058)

Filmer, D., King, E. M., & Pritchett, L. (1997).*Gender disparity in South Asia: Comparison between and within countries* (Policy research working paper).Washington, DC: World Bank.

Garcia-Retamero, R., & López-Zafra, E. (2006). Prejudice against women in male congenial environments: Perceptions of gender role congruity in leadership. *SexRoles, 55*(1-2), 51-61. doi:10.1007/s11199-006-9068-1

Gardenswartz, L., & Rowe, A. (2003).*Diverse team at work: Capitalizing on the power of diversity* (2nd ed.). Alexandria, VA: Society for Human Resources Management (SHRM).

Gathers, D. (2003). Diversity management: An imperative for healthcare organizations. *Hospital Topics, 81*(3), 14-20.

Gliner, J. A., & Morgan, G. A. (2000).*Research methods in applied settings: An integrated approach to design and analysis*. Mahwah, NJ: Lawrence Erlbaum.

Goussinsky, R., Reshef, A., Yanay-Ventura, G., &Yassour-Borochowitz, D. (2011). Teaching qualitative research for human services students: A three-phase model.*The Qualitative Report, 16*(1), 126-146.

Heathfield, S. M. (2013). Leadership rewards and recognition. *About.com Guide*.Retrieved from http://humanresources.about.com/od/leadership/a/leader_reward.htm

Hennink, M., Hutter, I., & Bailey, A. (2011).*Qualitative research methods*. Thousand Oaks, CA: Sage Publications.

Herzberg, F., Mausner, B., & Snyderman, B. B. (1959). *The motivation to work* (2nd ed.).New York, NY: John Wiley.

Hill, C. W. L. (2012). *International business: Competing in the global marketplace* (9thed.). New York, NY: McGraw-Hill/Irwin.

Hofstede, G., Hofstede, G. J., & Minkov, M. (2010). *Cultures and organizations: Software for the mind* (3rd ed.). New York, NY: McGraw-Hill Professional Publishing.

Horwitz, S. K. (2005). The compositional impact of team diversity on performance: Theoretical considerations. *Human Resource Development Review, 4*(2), 219-245.

Hur, Y., Strickland, R. A., & Stefanovic, D. (2010). Managing diversity: Does it matter to municipal governments? *The International Journal of Public Sector Management, 23*(5), 500-515. doi:10.1108/0951355101105850

Jackson, A. Y., &Mazzei, L. A. (2009).*Voice in qualitative inquiry: Challenging conventional, interpretive, and critical conceptions in qualitative research*. NewYork, NY: Routledge.

John, E. J., & William, L. B. (2001).Facilitating team development: A view from the field.*Group Facilitation, 3*, 56.

Kaiser, K. (2009). Protecting respondent confidentiality in qualitative research. *Qualitative Health Research, 19*, 1632.

Kandlousi, N. S. A. E., Ali, A. J., & Abdollahi, A. (2010). Organizational citizenship behavior in concern of communication satisfaction: The role of the formal and informal communication. *International Journal of Business and Management, 5*(10), 51-61.

Kapoor, C. (2011). Defining diversity: The evolution of diversity. *Worldwide Hospitality and Tourism Themes, 3*(4), 284-293. doi:10.1108/17554211111162408

Keyton, J., Caputo, J. M., Ford, E. A., Fu, R., Leibowitz, S. A., Liu, T., & Wu.C. (2013). Investigating verbal workplace communication behaviors.*Journal of Business Communication, 50*(2), 152-169.

Kim, B. Y. (2006). Managing workforce diversity: Developing a learning organization. *Organizational Journal of Human Resources in Hospitality & Tourism, 5*(2), 69-90.

Kvale, S. (2007). *Doing interviews*. Thousand Oaks, CA: Sage.

Lavinsky, D. (2012). *Start at the end: How companies can grow bigger and faster by reversing their business plan*. Hoboken, NJ: Wiley.

Lee, K. L., & Low, G. T. (2012). Leadership styles and organizational citizenship behavior: The mediating effect of subordinates' competence and downward influence tactics. *The Journal of Applied Business and Economics, 13*(2), 59-96.

Lewin, K., Lippitt, R., & White, R. K. (1939). Patterns of aggressive behavior in experimentally created "social climates." *Journal of Social Psychology, 10*, 271-299.

Lisowska, E. (2009). Gender diversity in the workplace.*Kobieta i Biznes,* 1-4, 42-46.

Litwin, M. S. (2003). *How to assess and interpret survey psychometrics* (2nd ed.).Thousand Oaks, CA: Sage.

Loden, M., & Rosener, J. B. (1991). *Workforce America! Managing employee diversity as a vital resource*. Homewood, IL: Business One Irwin.

Lowe, D., Levitt, K. J., & Wilson, T. (2011).Solutions for retaining Generation Y employees in the workplace.*Engineering Management, 39*(2), 46, 52.

Madden, M. P. (2008). *Women preparing for men's occupations: A phenomenology* (Doctoral dissertation). Retrieved from ProQuest Dissertations and Theses database. (3310937)

McClelland, D. (1988). *Human motivation*. New York, NY: Cambridge University Press.

McNamara, C. (2009). *General guidelines for conducting interviews.* Retrieved fromhttp://managementhelp.org/evaluatn/intrview.htm

Meister, J. C., &Willyerd, K. (2010).*The 2020 workplace: How innovative companies attract, develop, and keep tomorrow's employees today*. New York, NY:HarperBusiness.

Mihail, D. (2006). Gender-based stereotypes in the workplace: The case of Greece. *Equal Opportunities International, 25*(5), 373-388. doi:10.1108/02610150610706708

Mirza, A. M. B., & Jabeen, N. (2011). Gender stereotypes and women in management: The case of banking sector of Pakistan. *South Asian Studies, 26*(2), 259-284.

Murray, A. I. (1989). Top management group heterogeneity and firm performance. *Strategic Management Journal, 10*, 125-141. doi:10.1002/smj.4250100710

Newbury, J. (2011). Reflexivity in a study of family carers in home palliative care: A personal account. *Nurse Researcher, 19*(1), 30-36.

Norris, J. M., & Wylie, A. M. (2009, March). The evolving manager stereotype: The effects of industry gender typing on performance expectations for leaders and their teams. *Psychology of Women Quarterly, 33*, 419-428.

Ogbor, J. O. (2001). Critical theory and the hegemony of corporate culture. *Journal of Organizational Change Management, 14*(6), 590-608.

Oswald, D. P., &Coutinho, M. J. (2006). Why it matters: What is disproportionate representation? *The Special Edge, 20*(1), 1-4.

O'Toole, J. (2010, August). Leadership excellence essentials.*Journal of Leadership Education, 27*(8), 4.

Pajares, F., &Valiante, G. (2001). Gender differences in writing motivation and achievement of middle school students: A function of gender orientation?*Contemporary Educational Psychology, 26*(3), 366-381.

Polit, D., &Hungler, B. (1991).*Nursing research: Principles and methods.* New York,NY: JB Lippincott.

Popescu, M. (2013).Interpersonal communication relevance to professional development, in social systems.*International Journal of Academic Research in Business and Social Sciences, 3*(4), 370-375.

Powell, G. N. (2012). Six ways of seeing the elephant: The intersection of sex, gender, and leadership. *Gender in Management, 27*(2), 119-141. doi:10.1108/17542411211214167

Puryear, E. F. (1978, July 9). *Personal interview with Lieutenant General James V.Edmundson, USAF (Ret): 9 July 1978.* Montgomery, AL: Maxwell Air ForceBase.

Rai, S. (2012). Gender diversity in boardrooms: Comparative global review and India. *Journal of Strategic Human Resource Management, 1*(2), 16-24.

Rayudu, C. S. (2010). *Communication* (rev. ed.). Mumbai: Himalaya Publishing House.

RECOUP. (2008). *Reflexivity handout.* Retrieved fromhttp://manual.recoup.educ.cam.ac.uk/wiki/index.php/Qualitative_research/handout_on_reflexivity

Rijamampianina, R., & Carmichael, T. (2005, January). General issues in management: A pragmatic and holistic approach to managing diversity. *Problems and Perspectives in Management,* pp. 109-117.

Schmidt, J. (2014). *Gender diversity: Defining gender diversity.* Retrieved from http://www.TeAra.govt.nz/en/gender-diversity/page-1

Sethi, D., & Seth, M. (2009). Interpersonal communication: Lifeblood of an organization. *IUP Journal of Soft Skills, 3*(3), 32-40.

Sheard, A. G., & Kakabadse, A. P. (2004). A process perspective on leadership and team development. *Journal of Management Development, 23*(1), 7-106.

Shockley-Zalabak, P. (2011). *Fundamentals of organizational communication* (8th ed.). Upper Saddle River, NJ: Prentice Hall.

Thaver, B., & Mähick, P. (2008). Globalisation, diversity and academic practice: Reflections from South Africa and Sweden. *South African Review of Sociology, 39*(2).

Timony, B. C. (2006). *A qualitative research study on women faculty in higher education: Gender equity and commitment* (Doctoral dissertation). Retrieved fromProQuest Dissertations and Theses database. (3239895)

Trenka, J. (2006). Diversity in the work force: Challenges for employers. *Supervision; 67*(10), 17-21.

Triandis, H. C., & Wasti, S. A. (2008). Culture. In D. L. Stone, & E. F. Stone-Romero (Eds.), *The influence of culture on human resources management processes and practices* (pp. 1-24). New York, NY: Psychology Press.

Turner, D. W., III. (2010). Qualitative interview design: A practical guide for novice investigators. *The Qualitative Report, 15*(3), 754-760. Retrieved from http://www.nova.edu/ssss/QR/QR15-3/qid.pdf

Van Es, T. L. (2003, October). Defining corporate diversity. *Black Collegian, 34*, 51.

Wageeh, A. N., Nile, M. K., & Belal, A. K. (2012). Leadership styles and organizational learning: An empirical study on Saudi banks in Al-Taif Governorate Kingdom of Saudi Arabia. *Journal of Management and Strategy, 3*(1), 2.

Watts, J. H. (2008). Integrity in qualitative research. In L. M. Given (Ed.), *The Sage encyclopedia of qualitative research methods* (pp. 440-441). Thousand Oaks, CA:Sage Publications.

World Bank.(2001). *Nigeria University System Innovation Project*. Retrieved fromhttp://go.worldbank.org/OGJJMOKOU0

Printed in the United States
By Bookmasters